Developing Management Skills:

David A. Whetten
University of Illinois at Urbana-Champaign

Kim S. Cameron
University of Michigan

 HarperCollins*CollegePublishers*

Acquisitions Editor: Melissa A. Rosati
Project Coordination and Text Design: PC&F, Inc.
Cover Design: Kay Petronio
Production/Manufacturing: Michael Weinstein
Compositor: PC&F, Inc.
Printer and Binder: R.R. Donnelley & Sons Company
Cover Printer: Phoenix Color Corp.

Developing Management Skills: Solving Problems Creatively

Library of Congress Cataloging-in-Publication Data

Whetten, David A. (David Allred), 1946–
    Developing management skills : solving problems creatively /
David A. Whetten, Kim S. Cameron.
        p.   cm.
    Includes bibliographical references and index.
    ISBN 0-06-501793-5
    1. Management—Study and teaching.   2. Management—Problems,
exercises, etc.   I. Cameron, Kim S.   II. Title.
HD30.4.W465   1993
658.4'0071'173—dc20   92–46528
                                                        CIP

93 94 95 96 9 8 7 6 5 4 3 2 1

CONTENTS

PREFACE

We have been convinced for a decade or so that management skills must be a crucial part of the business school and executive education curriculum. Not only does the recent study of business education by Porter and McKibbin corroborate that view,[1] but our experience with business school students and managers in executive education seminars has continually reaffirmed our commitment to the need for a skills approach.

Originally, the motivation for writing *Developing Management Skills* grew out of our frustration with teaching management courses following conventional methods. When we used texts based on the traditional "principles of management" framework, we felt uncomfortable with their lack of theoretical and research grounding. Because principles of management have been generally derived from recollections and interpretations of practicing managers, empirical research and theory regarding their validity in organizations is limited.

When we used an organization and management theory approach, students and managers complained that the practical relevance of the material was difficult to discern. Not enough "how's" were included to be useful to individuals who aspired to improve their management competencies.

When we used a traditional "organizational behavior" approach, colleagues complained about redundancy. It became increasingly difficult to differentiate among topics covered by organizational behavior and management.

When we emphasized the "experiential learning" approach, centered around simulations, case discussions, and games, students and managers complained they weren't gaining enough substantive knowledge about how to be effective managers. Few students brought enough practical experience, theoretical knowledge, or self-analytic skills to those exercises to get much benefit from them, and managers thought the exercises were entertaining but not very useful.

After years of experimentation, we determined that while each approach had its place in a management program and each could contribute to an individual's education, none could, taken alone, help people develop into more competent managers.

In our search for alternatives, we asked several groups of people, from recent graduates to senior executives, to evaluate the organizational behavior and management curricula in terms of their experiences as managers. In general, they criticized behavioral science courses for not teaching them job-relevant skills. They were acutely aware of the challenges posed by "people problems" in their work, and they felt that their education had not prepared them for that component of their job.

Based on this feedback, we began formulating an approach for teaching management as a set of skills. In formulating the teaching methodology, we

[1] L. W. Porter and L. E. McKibbin, *Management Education and Development*. New York: McGraw-Hill, 1988.

examined the way such skills as education, social work, engineering, medicine and law are taught in other professional schools. We also drew heavily on recent innovations in training programs for practicing managers that emphasize behavior modification through role modeling. To identify the relevant management skills, we surveyed over 400 managers in public and private organizations and combed the professional literature for statements by management experts identifying the characteristics of effective managers. As our teaching model began to evolve, it became apparent that a supporting textbook would need to be developed. Further, it would necessarily have to be a hybrid, containing diverse teaching methods and material that would give equal emphasis to concept acquisition and skill practice.

Early in this project it was clear that our text would be at variance with prevailing views regarding what behavioral science courses should offer management students. Typically, these courses either present an array of general principles and concepts derived from research in industrial/organizational psychology, sociology, OB, industrial administration, and so on, or they rely heavily on group exercises, games, or cases to illustrate certain management activities. They either describe management practice and provide students with theories for analyzing common problems encountered by managers, or they eschew theory and research in favor of activity and involvement. Through our experience we became convinced that the strengths of each approach, used in combination, were needed for students to develop (not just know about) management skills. Therefore, the hallmark of this text is a balanced integration of theory and practice, understanding and application.

David A. Whetten

Kim S. Cameron

INTRODUCTION

THE CRITICAL ROLE OF MANAGEMENT SKILLS IN AMERICA'S FUTURE

For the first time in history, a book on management recently became this country's best seller. It has been succeeded by a host of additional books discussing management principles and organizational success stories that continue to sell hundreds of thousands of copies a year. Business services and organizational consulting have become the second most rapidly growing area in the U.S. service sector, lagging behind only health care services. Why has management suddenly become a hot topic in America? Why has so much attention been turned to the management of American organizations?

Our intent is not to try to duplicate the popular appeal of the best-selling books nor to utilize the common formula of recounting anecdotal incidents of successful organizations and managers. Rather, *Developing Management Skills* is a book designed specifically to help guide individuals in improving their own personal management competencies. It is more of a practicum and a guide to effective managerial behavior than a discussion of what someone else has done to successfully manage an organization.

We are making available each management skill covered in the *Developing Management Skills* book as a stand-alone module. Our intent is to make it possible for students and managers to supplement other educational or training expenditures with an in-depth focus on one particular skill. Before discussing the particular skill covered in this module, however, we want to review with you the central importance of developing management skills for success in organizations as well as in personal life.

We begin, therefore, by discussing the current conditions in American business. This helps illuminate the reason that competent management is such a critical concern right now. Then we discuss the extent to which effective management education and training are being provided by business schools and other executive training programs. The characteristics and qualities of successful managers derived from several research studies are summarized, and a model is presented that describes how these characteristics and qualities can best be developed.

CURRENT CONDITIONS IN AMERICAN BUSINESS

In approximately one decade, America's position as the undisputed world economic leader has been transformed into that of the world's largest debtor nation. In just five years (from 1981 to 1986) the U.S. went from a trade balance surplus to the largest trade deficit in the history of the world. Until recently most of that debt resulted from trade deficits in manufactured goods, but the same trend has recently come to characterize services as well. The service sector, which accounts for 71 percent of America's GNP and 75 percent of its jobs, experienced a trade deficit for the first time at the beginning of 1988.

The decline of U.S. business in a global environment has been dramatic and rapid. With the exception of nations that have been devastated by war, it is unlikely that any country has ever experienced as extensive and as rapid an economic decline as is currently underway in the United States. In 1986, for example, two-thirds of the net investment in the U.S. for housing, capital equipment, R&D, and plant construction was funded by foreign capital. Our biggest export, by far, has become IOUs. In every previous decade Americans consumed slightly less than 90 percent of what they produced, but since the beginning of the 1980s we have consumed 235 percent of our production growth. Only 30 percent of the growth in consumption over the last decade has been accounted for by increases in productivity. The other 70 percent was funded by cutbacks in domestic investment and foreign debt. Over the course of the 1980s, the U.S. investment rate was second lowest in the industrialized world, while the growth in output per worker was the absolute lowest. It took Britain seventy-five years to slide from the world's economic leader to second-class status by having productivity growth rates one-half a percentage point below competitor nations, but since the U.S. rate is three times lower than that, our slide is proceeding much more rapidly (see Peterson, 1987).

The number of business failures per 10,000 concerns has been at record levels since 1983, eclipsing the levels recorded during the Great Depression of 1929–1932. Since 1986, failure rates have been more than double those during the Depression. Failure rates in the service sector are also at record levels. Bank failures set all-time records yearly, the top 100 banks in the U.S. have not made a net profit for the past three years, and one bank a day is added to the problem-bank list by the FDIC. In the 1970s six of the largest ten banks in the world were American. In 1988 not a single U.S. bank is in the top twenty-five. Seventeen of the largest twenty-five banks are Japanese. Similarly, in 1979 eight of the largest public firms were American, but at the beginning of the 1990s only two made the list (the other eight are Japanese).

In the past fifteen years America has experienced a 25-percent decline in patent applications (innovations), and almost half of the U.S. patents awarded in 1986 and 1987 were to foreigners. The results of the decline in R&D investment in the U.S. is evidenced by a 1988 survey of opinions among top scientists. Most estimated that Japan will lead the world in R&D technology in the future with America well behind.

Consumers also demonstrate skepticism of American performance. A recent poll of American consumers asked which product they would buy if they knew that one brand was made in the U.S. and the other made in Japan. A majority said they would buy the Japanese product on the assumption that it would be of higher quality. One result of this skepticism is that, whereas America's standard of living was rated highest in the world until the mid-1970s, it now ranks fifth or below.

A variety of explanations and rationales have been proposed for this slide in U.S. business performance: for example, tax codes, restrictive trade barriers, and government regulations. However, most observers agree that at least part of the blame, and maybe even the lion's share of the blame, rests with America's managers.

Thurow (1984), for example, represents this point of view by asserting that there is a serious flaw in U.S. management:

> America is not experiencing a benevolent second industrial revolution, but a long-run economic decline that will affect its ability to competitively produce goods and services for world markets. If American industry fails, the managers are ultimately accountable. While we cannot fire all of America's managers any more than we can fire the American labor force, there is clearly something wrong with management. That something is going to have to be corrected if America is to compete in world markets.

Roy H. Pollock, former executive vice president at RCA, in 1987 characterized America's condition this way: "With the exception of the Civil War, it's doubtful that America has ever faced such an awesome trauma. Recovering from this situation won't be painless. But the alternative is to accept continuing economic decline and the end to America's greatness."

THE ROLE OF MANAGEMENT

Even in the face of these dismal indicators of economic performance and the threat of wrenching adjustments to be required of American businessmen, discouragement and resignation are neither appropriate nor predestined. There is reason to be hopeful. One reason for optimism is that there are no secrets regarding how to manage an effective firm or to turn around ineffective performance. There is no magic to competitiveness. Two scientific studies illustrate this point.

The first study was an investigation of the factors that best accounted for financial success over a five-year span in forty major manufacturing firms (Hanson, 1986). The question was, What explains the financial success of the firms that were winning? The five most powerful predictors were identified and assessed. They included marketshare (assuming that the higher the marketshare of a firm, the higher its profitability), firm capital intensity (assuming that the more a firm is automated and up-to-date in technology and equipment, the more profitable it is), size of the firm in assets (assuming that economies of scale and efficiency can be used in large firms to increase profitability), industry average return on sales (assuming that firms would reflect the performance of a highly profitable industry), and emphasis on management of human resources (assuming that an emphasis on good people management helps produce profitability in firms). The results of statistical analyses revealed that one factor—emphasis on the management of human resources—was three times more powerful than all other factors combined in accounting for firm financial success over a five-year period. Good "people management" was more important than all other factors in predicting profitability.

A second study was conducted by the U.S. Office of the Controller of the Currency (1987). It studied the reasons for the failures of national banks in the United States between 1979 and 1987. The total number of national banks that failed during that period was 162. Two major factors were found to account for the record number of bank failures during that eight-year period—distressed economic conditions and poor management. However, the relative impact of those two factors was somewhat surprising to the investigator. A total of 89 percent of the failed banks were judged to have had poor management. Only 35 percent of the failures had experienced depressed economic conditions in the region in which they operated, and in only 7 percent of the cases was a depressed economic condition the sole cause of bank failure. The government research team concluded:

> We found oversight and management deficiencies to be the primary factors that resulted in bank failure. In fact, poor policies, planning, and management were significant causes of failure in 89 percent of the banks surveyed. The quality of a bank's board and management depends on the experience, capability, judgment, and integrity of its directors and senior officers. Banks that had directors and managers with significant shortcomings made up a large portion of the banks that we surveyed.

These studies indicate that good management fosters financial success, while bad management fosters financial distress. Loss of firm competitiveness and financial decline are more products of shoddy management in U.S. firms than of macroeconomic factors or offshore price advantages.

This argument for the importance of good management for organization success is also supported by practical examples in two separate industries. Two different organizations recently underwent a change in top management, and the results produced by the introduction of a new management approach were dramatic. The first example comes from the General Motors automobile assembly plant in Fremont, California. The plant was built in the 1950s and, at the beginning of the 1980s, was assembling the Chevrolet Nova. The plant had a history of labor and productivity problems, however, and by the end of 1982 the performance statistics were dismal. Absenteeism was running at 20 percent. The number of formal grievances filed by employees totaled almost 5000 (that's an average of more than twenty grievances per day for every workday of the year!), and over 2000 grievances were still unresolved at year's end. An average of three to four wildcat strikes had been experienced during the previous few years, and both the productivity quantity and quality of production by the 5000 employees were the worst in the corporation. Costs of Fremont's Chevy Nova were about 30 percent above the Asian competitor's cars. In light of these data, corporate headquarters issued an order to close the plant and lay off the workers at the end of 1982.

In 1985, General Motors signed a joint operating agreement with one of its major competitors, Toyota. Much had been written about the Japanese method of managing, so General Motors asked Toyota to reopen and manage the Fremont plant. Most of the former U.S. auto workers were rehired, and the Japanese agreed to manage the plant. The primary difference between 1982 and 1985 was simply that a new management team was put in place; the workforce was essentially the same. At the end of 1986, in just one year's time, the performance data looked like this:

Absenteeism: 2 percent

Grievances: 2 outstanding

Strikes: None

Employees: 2500 (producing 20 percent more cars)

Productivity: Highest in the corporation

Quality: Highest in the corporation

Costs: Equal to those of the competition

The remarkable thing about this turnaround is that it did not take five or ten years to produce major improvements in productivity, cohesion, and commitment. It occurred in just over a year simply by changing the way workers were managed.

The second example involves a television manufacturing plant near Chicago. It was sold by its American owner to a Japanese company several years ago. Half of the white collar employees were let go, but the rest of the American workforce remained. In addition, the top management group was brought in from Japan. Essentially, the plant continued to produce the same product with the same workforce. The only difference was a new top management team. The difference between performance statistics under American management and Japanese management was dramatic. Under U.S. management, defects averaged 150 per 100 TV sets. Under Japanese management the average was 4. Product rejects averaged 60 per 100 TVs under U.S. management and only 3.8 under Japanese management. Warranty costs were $17 million per year with U.S. managers and $3 million with Japanese managers. In addition, productivity per day doubled under the new management team from 1000 sets per day to 2000 sets per day.

These illustrations point out, as Thurow and others assert, that management is a key factor in both firm success and firm failure. When excellent management is present, dramatic and rapid improvements can be effected. In surveys of CEOs, executives, and business owners, they consistently say that the factor most responsible for business failure is "bad management" and the best way to overcome business failures is to "provide better management." Of much less importance are factors such as interest rates, foreign competition, taxes, inflation, and government regulation. To the question, "What are the factors that are most important in overcoming business failure?", two answers outnumber all other responses: "Provide better managers," and "Train and educate current managers."

By using Japanese comparisons in the examples above, we do not intend to suggest that the Japanese management system is superior to the American system. We also emphasize that we are not suggesting that Japanese methods be adopted wholesale in American firms. In our own interviews with Japanese managers, many have explained their success by saying, "We just practice what you preach." Good management is not the prerogative of any single nationality or culture. Equally dramatic examples of firm and industry turnaround and excellence are prevalent in American firms with American managers: Xerox, IBM, Motorola, American Express, and Ford Motor, are a few examples. What we mean to point out is that changing the way managers behave in organizations can bring about quick and dramatic improvements. And preachments about how to do that have been around for a long time. Neither the Japanese nor any other culture has discovered many new principles that were not being advocated thirty years ago. The difference lies in the practice.

It is clear from the research and from these examples that the role of management in America's future is critical. What is less obvious, however, is what specifically constitutes "good" management. Questions such as what attributes and behaviors are displayed by effective managers and how an individual can learn to be a good manager are still left unaddressed. The identification of attributes of effective management and the teaching of management to individuals has been the role accepted by business schools and management education programs. The trouble is, this role has not been performed as effectively as it might have been.

MANAGEMENT EDUCATION

For the past decade, management education in America has been assailed as a culprit in contributing to this country's economic decline. This criticism has most often been aimed at business schools and other management education programs. Over 200 articles have appeared in the last decade in a wide array of academic and popular publications with such titles as "Managing Our Way to Economic Decline," "Overhauling America's Business Management," "The Failure of Business Education," "The Crisis in Business Education," "Are Business Schools Doing Their Job?", "Business Schools and Their Critics," and "What Good are B-Schools?" The criticisms are pointed. For example, Donald E. Peterson (1990) asserted: "The business schools . . . are doing more harm than good. I no longer flippantly say, as I used to, 'close their doors,' because now I'm beginning to believe that maybe this idea has serious merit." Wrapp (1982: 35) added: "Business schools have done more to ensure the success of the Japanese and West German invasion of America than any one thing I can think of." Samuelson (1990) stated simply: "For three decades we've run an experiment on the social utility of business schools. They've flunked. If they were improving the quality of U.S. management, the results ought to be obvious by now. They aren't."

Even the American Assembly of Collegiate Schools of Business (1985), the accreditation agency for America's business schools, admitted:

> In recent years, as the U.S. seems to have lost its edge in worldwide industrial competitiveness, nearly every sector of society has criticized U.S. corporate management. Critics say that the U.S. manager is short-term oriented, naively quantitative, averse to risk, self-centered, deficient in ethics and loyalty, impatient for promotion, overpriced, and unconcerned with real productivity. Not all managers fit such descriptions by any means. But enough apparently do to prompt the question, how did they become that way? What kind of managers are the business schools and other management development programs producing?

Pfeffer (1981) argued that the main problem in business schools and management education is the type of training imparted:

> . . . management education or performance in management schools does not predict subsequent career success for managers. But why not? It is because of the type of training imparted. Management schools impart both the ideology and skills of analysis. . . . Optimization techniques for the core of current courses. . . . Students emerge from such a program believing that there is an optimal answer or set of answers discoverable through quantitative analysis.

Mintzberg (1987) expressed a similar point of view:

> Ideal management education should reorient its priorities. My ideal
> management training would emphasize skill training, experiential education,
> if you like. Perhaps forty percent of the effort should be devoted to it. . . .
> A great deal is known about inculcating such skills. But not in the business
> schools.

Scientific data support the assertions of these and other authors that, in the absence of skill training, performance in school is not predictive of subsequent career success. Cohen (1984) summarized the results of 108 studies of the relationship between performance in college courses (as measured by grade-point average) and subsequent life success. Life success was measured in these studies by a variety of factors, including job performance, income, promotions, personal satisfaction, eminence, and graduate degrees. The mean correlation between performance in school and performance in life in these 108 studies was .18, and in no case did the correlation exceed .20. These low correlations suggest that school performance and successful performance in subsequent life activities are related only marginally.

What is the explanation for these dismal results? Why strive hard to achieve in formal education programs? Do grades matter at all? Should students and executives invest in formal education and training to try to improve their managerial competencies, or can good management be learned on the job? Should anyone go into debt to attend a business school?

Obviously, we believe that formal education and management training can positively affect managerial performance. We also believe that there must be a concerted effort to help develop such management talent in order to foster turnaround and excellence in American firms. Those beliefs, however, are not based on blind optimism. Scientific evidence exists that such training can make a difference both to an individual and to the bottom-line performance of a firm. We summarize two studies below that provide support for this contention. First, however, we must address the question, "What constitutes effective management?" Then we can discuss how formal education can help one improve management competence and the extent to which improvement will affect the performance of an organization.

EFFECTIVE MANAGEMENT

In an effort to identify what constitutes effective management, we conducted an investigation in which we identified individuals who were rated as highly effective managers in their own organizations. We contacted organizations in the fields of business, health care, education, and state government and asked senior officers to name the most effective managers in their organizations. We then interviewed these people to determine what attributes they associated with managerial effectiveness. We also reviewed studies done by other researchers that attempted to identify the characteristics of effective managers.

In our own study, 402 highly effective managers were identified by their peers and superiors in this sample of organizations. We interviewed these individuals and tried to discover what made them such successful managers. Among the questions were:

- How have you become so successful in this organization?
- Who fails and who succeeds in this organization and why?
- If you had to train someone to take your place, what knowledge and what skills would you make certain that person possessed?
- If you could design an ideal course or training program to teach you to be a better manager, what would it contain?
- Think of other effective managers you know. What skills do they demonstrate that explain their success?

Our analysis of the interviews produced about sixty characteristics of effective managers. The ten identified most often are listed in Table 1. Notice that these ten characteristics are all behavioral skills. They are not personality attributes or styles, nor are they generalizations such as "luck" or "timing." They also are not very surprising. The characteristics of effective managers, we concluded, are not a secret.

The attributes derived from our study are similar to those resulting from several other surveys published in the management literature. Table 2, for example, lists the results of several studies using a variety of kinds of respondents. Not surprisingly, the two lists are highly similar. Regardless of whether respondents are CEOs or first-line supervisors, whether they work in the public sector or the private sector, their skills are generally well marked and agreed upon by observers. It is not hard to identify and describe the skills of effective managers.

Three notable characteristics are typical of most of these skills. First, the skills are behavioral. They are not personality attributes or stylistic tendencies. They consist of an identifiable set of actions that individuals perform and that lead to certain outcomes. An important implication, therefore, is that individuals can learn to perform these actions or can improve their current level of performance. Whereas people with different styles and personalities may apply the skills differently, there is, nevertheless, a core set of observable attributes of effective skill performance that are common across a range of individual differences.

Table 1.1

The Most Frequently Cited Skills of Effective Managers

1. Verbal communication (including listening)
2. Managing time and stress
3. Managing individual decisions
4. Recognizing, defining, and solving problems
5. Motivating and influencing others
6. Delegating
7. Setting goals and articulating a vision
8. Self-awareness
9. Team building
10. Managing conflict

Table 1.2 Identifying Critical Management Skills: A Sample of Studies

■ STUDY ■ RESPONDENTS ■ FOCUS	RESULTS	
■ Prentice (1984) ■ 230 executives in manufacturing, retail, and service firms ■ Critical skills for managing organizations	Listening Communication Leadership Problem solving Time management Adaptability to change	Interpersonal relations Formal presentations Stress management
■ Margerison & Kakabadse (1984) ■ 721 chief executive officers in U.S. corporations ■ Most important things you've learned in order to be a chief executive	(1) Communication Managing people Delegation Patience Respect Control Understanding people Evaluating personnel Tolerance Team spirit	(2) Strategic planning Decision making Self-discipline Analytic abilities Hard work Flexibility Financial management Time management Knowledge of the business Clear thinking
■ Margerison & Kakabadse (1984) ■ 721 chief executive officers in U.S. corporations ■ Key management skills to develop in others to help them become senior executives	Human relations Communication Planning and goal setting People management and leadership	Decision making Financial management Entrepreneurial skills Delegating Broad experience Teamwork
■ Cameron & Whetten (1984) ■ 50 consultants, professors, management development experts, and public administrators ■ Critical management skills needed by state government managers	Managing conflict Motivating others Managing stress and time Decision making Delegation	Goal setting Problem solving Designing jobs Gaining and using power Career planning
■ Hunsicker (1978) ■ 1854 Air Force officers ■ Skills that most contribute to successful management	Communication Human relations General management ability Technical competence	Leadership Knowledge and experience

Table I.2   (Continued)

■ Luthans, Rosenkrantz, & Hennessey (1985) ■ 52 managers in 3 organizations ■ Participant observation of skills demonstrated by most effective versus least effective managers	Managing conflict Building power and influence Communicating with outsiders	Decision making Communicating with insiders Developing subordinates Processing paperwork Planning and goal setting
■ Benson (1983) ■ A survey of 25 studies in business journals ■ A summary of the skills needed by students entering the professions	Listening Written communication Oral communication Motivating/persuading	Interpersonal skills Informational interviewing Group problem solving
■ Curtis, Winsor, & Stephens (1989) ■ 428 members of the American Society of Personnel Administrators in the United States ■ (1) Skills needed to obtain employment, (2) skills important for successful job performance, and (3) skills needed to move up in the organization	(1) Verbal communication Listening Enthusiasm Written communication Technical competence Appearance	(2) Interpersonal skills Verbal communication Written communication Persistence/determination Enthusiasm Technical competence
	(3) Ability to work well with others one-on-one Ability to gather information and make a decision Ability to work well in groups Ability to listen and give counsel Ability to give effective feedback Ability to write effective reports Knowledge of the job	Ability to present a good image for the firm Ability to use computers Knowledge of management theory Knowledge of finance Knowledge of marketing Knowledge of accounting Ability to use business machines.

A second characteristic is that these skills seem, in several cases, to be contradictory or paradoxical. For example, they are neither all soft and humanistic in orientation nor all hard-driving and directive. They are oriented neither toward teamwork and interpersonal relations exclusively nor toward individualism and entrepreneurship exclusively. A variety of types of skills are present.

To illustrate, Cameron and Tschirhart (1988) assessed the skill performance of over 500 mid-level and upper middle managers in about 150 organizations. They used the twenty-five most frequently mentioned management skills taken from those in Tables 1 and 2 as well as from research by Ghiselli, (1963), Livingston (1971), Miner (1973), Katz (1974), Mintzberg (1975), Flanders (1981), and Boyatzis (1982). Through statistical analyses it was discovered that the skills could be sorted into four main groups. One group of skills focused on participative and human relations skills (for example, supportive communication and teambuilding), while another group focused on just the opposite, that is, on competitiveness and control (for example, assertiveness, power, and influence skills). A third group focused on innovativeness and entrepreneurship (such as creative problem solving), while a fourth group emphasized quite the opposite type of skills, namely maintaining order and rationality (for example, managing time and rational decision making).

One conclusion from that study was that effective managers are required to demonstrate paradoxical skills. That is, the most effective managers are both participative and hard-driving, both nurturing and competitive. They were able to be flexible and creative while also being controlled, stable, and rational. The second characteristic associated with effective management, then, is the mastery of diverse and seemingly contradictory skills.

Third, these critical skills were interrelated and overlapping. No effective manager performed one skill or one set of skills independent of others. For example, in order to effectively motivate others, skills such as supportive communication, influence, and delegation were also required. Effective managers, therefore, develop a constellation of skills that overlap and support one another and that allow flexibility in managing diverse situations.

IMPROVING MANAGEMENT SKILLS

Successful management, of course, is more than just following a cookbook list of sequential behaviors. Developing highly competent management skills is much more complicated than developing skills such as those associated with a trade (e.g., welding) or a sport (e.g., shooting baskets). Management skills are (1) linked to a more complex knowledge base than other types of skills and (2) inherently connected to interaction with other (frequently unpredictable) individuals. A standardized approach to welding or shooting baskets may be feasible, but no standardized approach to managing human beings is possible.

On the other hand, what all skills do have in common is the potential for improvement through practice. Any approach to developing management skills, therefore, must involve a heavy dose of practical application. At the same time, practice without the necessary conceptual knowledge is sterile and ignores the need for flexibility and adaptation to different situations. Therefore, developing skill competency is inherently tied to both conceptual learning and behavioral practice.

The method we have found to be most successful in helping individuals develop management skills is based on social learning theory (Bandura, 1977; Davis & Luthans, 1980). This approach marries rigorous conceptual knowledge with opportunities to practice and apply observable behaviors. Variations on this general approach have been used widely in on-the-job supervisory training programs (Goldstein & Sorcher, 1974), as well as in allied professional education classrooms such as teacher development and social work (Rose, Crayner, & Edleson, 1977; Singleton, Spurgeon, & Stammers, 1980).

This learning model, as originally formulated, consists of four steps: (1) the presentation of behavioral principles or action guidelines, generally using traditional instruction methods; (2) demonstration of the principles by means of cases, films, scripts, or incidents; (3) opportunities to practice the principles through role plays or exercises; and (4) feedback on performance from peers, instructors, or experts. Our own experience in teaching complex management skills has convinced us that three important modifications are necessary in order for this model to be most effective. First, the behavioral principles must be grounded in social science theory and in reliable research results. Commonsense generalizations and panacea-like prescriptions appear regularly in the popular management literature. To ensure the validity of the behavioral guidelines being prescribed, the learning approach must include scientifically based knowledge about the effects of the management principles being presented.

Second, individuals must be aware of their current level of skill competency and be motivated to improve upon that level in order to benefit from the model. Most people receive very little feedback about their current level of competency in most skill areas. Most organizations provide some kind of annual or semi-annual evaluation (for example, course grades in school or performance appraisal interviews in firms), but these evaluations are almost always infrequent, are rather narrow in scope, and do not assess performance in most critical skill areas. To help a person understand what skills to improve and why, therefore, a preassessment activity must be part of the model.

In addition, most people find change rather uncomfortable and, therefore, avoid taking the risk to develop new behavior patterns. A preassessment activity in the learning model helps encourage these people to change by illuminating their strengths and weaknesses. A person then knows where weaknesses lie and what needs to be improved. Preassessment activities generally take the form of self-evaluation instruments, case studies, or problems that help highlight personal strengths and weaknesses in a particular skill area.

Third, a back-home application component is needed in the learning model. Most management skill training takes place in a classroom setting where feedback is immediate and it is relatively safe to try out new behaviors and make mistakes. Therefore, transferring learning to the job is often problematic. Application exercises help to apply classroom learning to examples from the real world of management. Application exercises often take the form of an outside-of-class intervention, or consulting assignment, or a problem-centered intervention, which the student then analyzes to determine its degree of success or failure.

In sum, evidence suggests that a five-step learning model is most effective for helping individuals develop management skills (see Cameron & Whetten, 1983; Whetten & Cameron, 1983). It is outlined in Table 3. Step 1 involves the preassessment of current levels of skill competency and knowledge of the behavioral principles. Step 2 consists of the presentation of validated, scientifically-based principles and guidelines for effective skill performance. Step 3 is an analysis step in which models or cases are made available in order to analyze the behavioral principles in real organizational settings. This step also helps demonstrate how the behavioral guidelines can be adapted to different personal styles and circumstances. Step 4 consists of practice exercises in which experimentation can occur and immediate feedback can be received in a relatively safe environment. Finally, step 5 is the application of the skill to a real-life setting outside the classroom with follow-up analysis of the relative success of that application.

Research on the effectiveness of training programs using this general learning model has shown that it produces results superior to those based on the traditional lecture-discussion approach (Moses & Ritchie, 1976; Burnaska, 1976; Smith, 1976; Latham & Saari, 1979; Porras & Anderson, 1981). In addition, evidence suggests that management skill training can have significant impact on the bottom-line performance of a firm. For example, the U.S. Postal Service completed a study a few years ago in which 49 of the largest 100 post offices in America were evaluated. An important question in the study was, "How can we make post offices more effective?" Productivity and service quality were both monitored over a period of five years. The two major factors that had impact on these effectiveness measures were (1) degree of mechanization (automation), and (2) investment in training. Two kinds of training were provided: maintenance training (training in operating and maintaining the equipment) and management training (training in developing management skills). The overall conclusion of the study was, "Performance

Table 1.3 A Model for Developing Management Skills

COMPONENTS	CONTENTS	OBJECTIVES
Skill preassessment	Survey instruments Role plays	Assess current level of skill competence and knowledge; create readiness to change.
Skill learning	Written text Behavorial guidelines	Teach correct principles and present a rationale for behavioral guidelines.
Skill analysis	Cases	Provide examples of appropriate and inappropriate skill performance. Analyze behavioral principles and reasons they work.
Skill practice	Exercises Simulations Role plays	Practice behavioral guidelines. Adapt principles to personal style. Receive feedback and assistance.
Skill application	Assignments (behavioral and written)	Transfer classroom learning to real-life situations. Foster ongoing personal development.

levels in these organizations vary systematically and predictably as training levels vary. The training-performance relationship is positive and statistically significant." More specifically, the study found that (1) providing management training was more important than providing maintenance training in accounting for improved productivity and service in the post offices, and (2) both kinds of training were more important than having automated or up-to-date equipment in the post office (mechanization). Low-tech offices outperformed high-tech offices when managers were provided with management skill training. In sum, its five-year study convinced the U.S. Postal Service that helping employees to develop management skills was the best way to improve organizational effectiveness.

The point we are emphasizing is that management skill training is a critical developmental activity for both potential and practicing managers. We have provided evidence that many American organizations are in great danger of losing their competitiveness to offshore firms as well as their credibility here at home. Moreover, evidence suggests that it is, to a significant extent, the managers who are at fault. To improve management, and thereby to improve organizational performance, we suggest that one important activity is training more managers in critical management skills. Mintzberg (1975, p. 60) made a similar point several years ago:

> Management schools will begin the serious training of managers when skill training takes its place next to cognitive learning. Cognitive learning is detached and informational, like reading a book or listening to a lecture. No doubt much important cognitive material must be assimilated by the manager-to-be. But cognitive learning no more makes a manager than it does a swimmer. The latter will drown the first time he jumps into the water if his coach never takes him out of the lecture hall, gets him wet, and gives him feedback on his performance. Our management schools need to identify the skills managers use, select students who show potential in these skills, put the students into situations where these skills can be practiced, and then give them systematic feedback on their performance.

More recently, Porter and McKibbin (1988), after completing a study of management education in American business schools sponsored by the American Assembly of Collegiate Schools of Business, concluded:

> The challenge of how to develop stronger people skills needs to be faced by both business schools in the education of their degree program students and by corporations and firms in their management development activities.

Donald E. Peterson (1990), recently retired chairman and CEO at Ford Motor Company, agreed: "The element that is still not as well-instilled as I might wish is the importance of people skills in being a successful manager. Most schools still stress individual performance."

These perspectives match those of our own students and colleagues in business organizations who, based on their own personal experience and observations, have reached the same conclusions. For example, one vice president of a major computer manufacturer observed:

Many management school graduates have a hard time adjusting to organizational reality. They are long on analytic skills and short on implementation skills. The best solution in the world is worthless unless you can get others to support it. We call this malady "paralysis by analysis."

A partner in a "Big Eight" accounting firm similarly observed:

The higher up the organization you go, the less relevant technical knowledge becomes. It is important for your first couple of promotions, but after that, people skills are what count.

A recent graduate from a Big Ten management school also reported:

I can't believe it. I went for my second interview with a company last week, and I spent the first half-day participating in simulation exercises with ten other job candidates. They videotaped me playing the role of a salesman handling an irate customer, a new director of personnel putting down a revolt by the "old guard," and a plant manager trying to convince people of the need to install a radically new production process. Boy, was I unprepared for that!

The message behind these personal observations is clear—from all perspectives, competence in interpersonal skills is a critical prerequisite for success in management. Strong analytical and quantitative skills are important, but they are not sufficient. Successful managers must be able to work effectively with people. Unfortunately, interpersonal and management skills have not always been a high priority for business school students and aspiring executives. In a survey of 110 Fortune 500 CEOs, 87 percent were satisfied with the level of competence and analytic skills of business school graduates, 68 percent were satisfied with conceptual skills of graduates, but only 43 percent of the CEOs were satisfied with graduates' management skills, and only 28 percent were satisfied with their interpersonal skills!

DEVELOPING A MANAGEMENT SKILL

The management skill that follows is one that research has identified as crucial for managerial success. It is one of several important management skills discussed in the book, *Developing Management Skills*. This module contains only one of these skills.

The management skills covered in the book *Developing Management Skills* are (1) Developing Self-Awareness, (2) Managing Stress, (3) Solving Problems Creatively, (4) Communicating Supportively, (5) Gaining Power and Influence, (6) Motivating Others, (7) Managing Conflict, and (8) Conducting Meetings, Making Oral Presentations, and Interviewing.

Appendix I contains scoring keys and forms for use with assignments in the chapters; **Appendix II** is a glossary of key terms in the text; and **Appendix III** lists references for excerpted material in the book.

Our discussion of each skill is organized on the basis of the learning model summarized in Table 3 on page 13. The discussion begins with **Skill Preassessment** instruments. Their purpose is to help you focus attention on areas of personal competence as well as areas needing improvement in both knowledge and performance.

An explanation of the key behavioral guidelines, as well as a rationale for why these guidelines work, is found in the **Skill Learning** section. The purpose of this section is to explain the core behavioral principles associated with each skill. We present a model of each skill along with evidence from research that the principles identified are effective in practice. Our objective is to provide a sound rationale for the action guidelines summarized at the end of the section.

In the **Skill Analysis** section, you will find brief case histories that illustrate both effective and ineffective applications of the behavioral principles. The purpose of this section is to bridge the gap between intellectual understanding and behavioral application. Critiquing a manager's performance in a real-life case enhances your understanding of the skill learning material. Each case provides a model of effective performance and helps identify ways that the skill can be adapted to personal style.

The **Skill Practice** section provides exercises, problems, and role-play assignments. The goal of this section is to provide opportunities to practice the behavioral guidelines in simulated managerial situations and to receive feedback from peers and instructors. Practicing these managerial skills in a classroom setting is not only safer and less costly than in a real-life management job, but others' observation and feedback can be more precise and more timely as well.

The last section of each skill discussion is the **Skill Application** section. It contains a form for helping you generate your own improvement agenda as well as assignments and ideas for applying the skill in an out-of-class situation. The purpose of these assignments is to help you transfer the behavioral guidelines into everyday practice. You may be directed to teach the skill to someone else, to consult with another manager to help resolve a relevant problem, or to apply the skill in an ongoing organization or a family.

CONCLUSION

In conclusion, *Developing Management Skills* is not intended just for individuals who are planning to enter managerial jobs or who are currently managing organizations. It is intended to help people in general better manage many aspects of their lives and relationships. In fact, John Holt (1964, p. 165) summarized our intention succinctly by equating management skill to intelligence:

> When we talk about intelligence, we do not mean the ability to get a good score on a certain kind of test or even the ability to do well in school; these are at best only indicators of something larger, deeper and far more important. By intelligence we mean a style of life, a way of behaving in various situations. The true test of intelligence is not how much we know how to do, but how we behave when we don't know what to do.

Fostering the development of such intelligence is the goal of *Developing Management Skills*.

Developing
Management Skills:
Solving Problems Creatively

SOLVING PROBLEMS CREATIVELY

Skill Development Objectives

To increase proficiency in

- rational problem solving
- recognizing personal conceptual blocks
- enhancing creativity by overcoming conceptual blocks
- fostering innovation among others

PERSONAL SKILLS

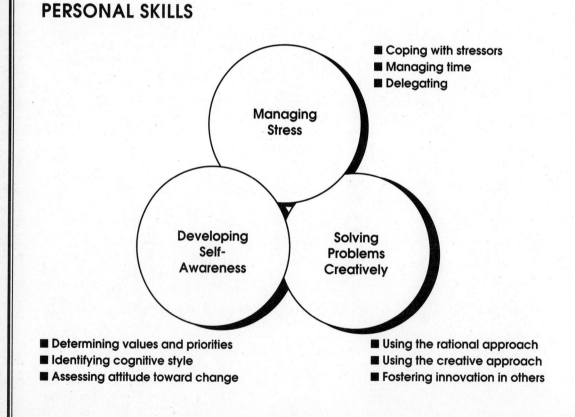

■ Coping with stressors
■ Managing time
■ Delegating

Managing Stress

Developing Self-Awareness

Solving Problems Creatively

■ Determining values and priorities
■ Identifying cognitive style
■ Assessing attitude toward change

■ Using the rational approach
■ Using the creative approach
■ Fostering innovation in others

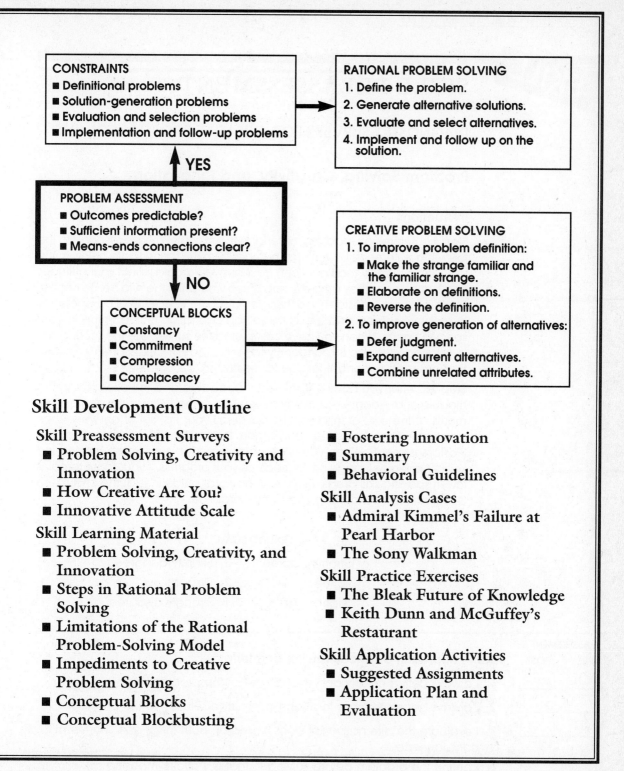

CONSTRAINTS
- Definitional problems
- Solution-generation problems
- Evaluation and selection problems
- Implementation and follow-up problems

RATIONAL PROBLEM SOLVING
1. Define the problem.
2. Generate alternative solutions.
3. Evaluate and select alternatives.
4. Implement and follow up on the solution.

YES

PROBLEM ASSESSMENT
- Outcomes predictable?
- Sufficient information present?
- Means-ends connections clear?

NO

CREATIVE PROBLEM SOLVING
1. To improve problem definition:
   - Make the strange familiar and the familiar strange.
   - Elaborate on definitions.
   - Reverse the definition.
2. To improve generation of alternatives:
   - Defer judgment.
   - Expand current alternatives.
   - Combine unrelated attributes.

CONCEPTUAL BLOCKS
- Constancy
- Commitment
- Compression
- Complacency

Skill Development Outline

Skill Preassessment Surveys
- Problem Solving, Creativity and Innovation
- How Creative Are You?
- Innovative Attitude Scale

Skill Learning Material
- Problem Solving, Creativity, and Innovation
- Steps in Rational Problem Solving
- Limitations of the Rational Problem-Solving Model
- Impediments to Creative Problem Solving
- Conceptual Blocks
- Conceptual Blockbusting

- Fostering Innovation
- Summary
- Behavioral Guidelines

Skill Analysis Cases
- Admiral Kimmel's Failure at Pearl Harbor
- The Sony Walkman

Skill Practice Exercises
- The Bleak Future of Knowledge
- Keith Dunn and McGuffey's Restaurant

Skill Application Activities
- Suggested Assignments
- Application Plan and Evaluation

SKILL PREASSESSMENT

SKILL

DIAGNOSTIC SURVEYS FOR CREATIVE PROBLEM SOLVING

Problem Solving, Creativity, and Innovation

Instructions

Step 1: Before you read the material in this module, please respond to the following statements by writing a number from the rating scale below in the left-hand column (Preassessment). Your answers should reflect your attitudes and behavior as they are *now*, not as you would *like* them to be. Be honest. This instrument is designed to help you discover your level of competency in problem solving and creativity so you can tailor your learning to your specific needs. When you have completed the survey, use the scoring key in Appendix I, page 84, to identify the skill areas discussed in this module that are most important for you to master.

Step 2: After you have completed the reading and the exercises in this module and—ideally—as many as you can of the Skill Application assignments at the end of this module, cover up your first set of answers. Then respond to the same statements again, this time in the right-hand column (Postassessment). When you have completed the survey, use the scoring key in Appendix I, page 84, to measure your progress. If your score remains low in specific skill areas, use the behavioral guidelines at the end of the Skill Learning section to guide further practice.

RATING SCALE

6 Strongly agree   3 Slightly disagree

5 Agree   2 Disagree

4 Slightly agree   1 Strongly disagree

ASSESSMENT

PRE-   POST-   **When I approach a typical, routine problem,**

_____ _____   1. I always define clearly and explicitly what the problem is.

_____ _____   2. I always generate more than one alternative solution to the problem.

_____ _____   3. I evaluate the alternative solutions based on both long- and short-term consequences.

_____ _____   4. I define the problem before solving it; that is, I avoid imposing my predetermined solutions on problems.

_____ _____ 5. I keep problem-solving steps distinct; that is, I make sure to separate formulating definitions, generating alternatives, and finding solutions.

When faced with a complex or difficult problem that does not have a straightforward solution,

_____ _____ 6. I try to define the problem in several different ways.

_____ _____ 7. I try to be flexible in the way I approach the problem; I don't just rely on conventional wisdom or past practice.

_____ _____ 8. I look for patterns or common elements in different aspects of the problem.

_____ _____ 9. I try to unfreeze my thinking by asking lots of questions about the nature of the problem.

_____ _____ 10. I try to apply both the left (logical) side of my brain and the right (intuitive) side of my brain to the problem.

_____ _____ 11. I frequently use metaphors or analogies to help me analyze the problem and discover what else it is like.

_____ _____ 12. I strive to look at problems from different perspectives so as to generate multiple definitions.

_____ _____ 13. I do not evaluate the merits of an alternative solution to the problem until I have generated other alternatives.

_____ _____ 14. I often break the problem down into smaller components and analyze each one separately.

_____ _____ 15. I strive to generate multiple creative solutions to problems.

When trying to foster more creativity and innovation among those with whom I work,

_____ _____ 16. I help arrange opportunities for individuals to work on their ideas outside the constraints of normal procedures.

_____ _____ 17. I make sure there are divergent points of view represented in every problem-solving group.

_____ _____ 18. I sometimes make outrageous suggestions, even demands, to help stimulate people to find new ways of approaching problems.

_____ _____ 19. I try to acquire information from customers regarding their preferences and expectations.

_____ _____ 20. I sometimes involve outsiders (for example, customers or recognized experts) in problem-solving discussions.

_____ _____ 21. I provide recognition not only to those who are idea champions but also to those who support others' ideas and who provide resources to implement them.

_____ _____ 22. I encourage informed rule-breaking in pursuit of creative solutions.

How Creative Are You?©(REVISED)

How creative are you? The following test helps you determine if you have the personality traits, attitudes, values, motivations and interests that make up creativity. It is based on several years' study of attributes possessed by men and women in a variety of fields and occupations who think and act creatively.

Instructions

For each statement, write in the appropriate letter:

A = Agree
B = Undecided or Don't Know
C = Disagree

Be as frank as possible. Try not to second-guess how a creative person might respond.

Scoring: Turn to Appendix I, page 84, to find the answer key and an interpretation of your scores.

_____ 1. I always work with a great deal of certainty that I am following the correct procedure for solving a particular problem.

_____ 2. It would be a waste of time for me to ask questions if I had no hope of obtaining answers.

_____ 3. I concentrate harder on whatever interests me than do most people.

_____ 4. I feel that a logical step-by-step method is best for solving problems.

_____ 5. In groups I occasionally voice opinions that seem to turn some people off.

_____ 6. I spend a great deal of time thinking about what others think of me.

_____ 7. It is more important for me to do what I believe to be right than to try to win the approval of others.

_____ 8. People who seem uncertain about things lose my respect.

_____ 9. More than other people, I need to have things interesting and exciting.

_____ 10. I know how to keep my inner impulses in check.

_____ 11. I am able to stick with difficult problems over extended periods of time.

_____ 12. On occasion I get overly enthusiastic.

_____ 13. I often get my best ideas when doing nothing in particular.

_____ 14. I rely on intuitive hunches and the feeling of ''rightness'' or ''wrongness'' when moving toward the solution of a problem.

_____ 15. When problem solving, I work faster when analyzing the problem and slower when synthesizing the information I have gathered.

_____ 16. I sometimes get a kick out of breaking the rules and doing things I am not supposed to do.

_____ 17. I like hobbies that involve collecting things.

_____ 18. Daydreaming has provided the impetus for many of my more important projects.

_____ 19. I like people who are objective and rational.

_____ 20. If I had to choose from two occupations other than the one I now have, I would rather be a physician than an explorer.

_____ 21. I can get along more easily with people if they belong to about the same social and business class as myself.

_____ 22. I have a high degree of aesthetic sensitivity.

_____ 23. I am driven to achieve high status and power in life.

_____ 24. I like people who are most sure of their conclusions.

_____ 25. Inspiration has nothing to do with the successful solution of problems.

_____ 26. When I am in an argument, my greatest pleasure would be for the person who disagrees with me to become a friend, even at the price of sacrificing my point of view.

_____ 27. I am much more interested in coming up with new ideas than in trying to sell them to others.

_____ 28. I would enjoy spending an entire day alone, just ''chewing the mental cud.''

_____ 29. I tend to avoid situations in which I might feel inferior.

_____ 30. In evaluating information, the source is more important to me than the content.

_____ 31. I resent things being uncertain and unpredictable.

_____ 32. I like people who follow the rule, ''business before pleasure.''

_____ 33. Self-respect is much more important than the respect of others.

_____ 34. I feel that people who strive for perfection are unwise.

_____ 35. I prefer to work with others in a team effort rather than solo.

_____ 36. I like work in which I must influence others.

_____ 37. Many problems that I encounter in life cannot be resolved in terms of right or wrong solutions.

_____ 38. It is important for me to have a place for everything and everything in its place.

_____ 39. Writers who use strange and unusual words merely want to show off.

_____ 40. Below is a list of terms that describe people. Choose 10 words that best characterize you.

☐ energetic	☐ alert
☐ persuasive	☐ curious
☐ observant	☐ organized
☐ fashionable	☐ unemotional
☐ self-confident	☐ clear-thinking
☐ persevering	☐ understanding
☐ original	☐ dynamic
☐ cautious	☐ self-demanding
☐ habit-bound	☐ polished
☐ resourceful	☐ courageous
☐ egotistical	☐ efficient
☐ independent	☐ helpful
☐ stern	☐ perceptive
☐ predictable	☐ quick
☐ formal	☐ good-natured
☐ informal	☐ thorough
☐ dedicated	☐ impulsive
☐ forward-looking	☐ determined
☐ factual	☐ realistic
☐ open-minded	☐ modest
☐ tactful	☐ involved
☐ inhibited	☐ absent-minded
☐ enthusiastic	☐ flexible
☐ innovative	☐ sociable
☐ poised	☐ well-liked
☐ acquisitive	☐ restless
☐ practical	☐ retiring

SOURCE: Eugene Raudsepp, President, Princeton Creative Research, Inc.

Innovative Attitude Scale

Please indicate the extent to which each of the statements on the opposite page is true of either your *actual* behavior or your *intentions* at work. That is, describe the way you are or the way you intend to be on the job. Use the following scale for your responses:

5—Almost always true

4—Often true

3—Not applicable

2—Seldom true

1—Almost never true

Scoring: To score the "Innovative Attitude Scale" turn to Appendix I, page 86, to find the answer key and an interpretation of your score.

———— 1. I openly discuss with my boss how to get ahead.

———— 2. I try new ideas and approaches to problems.

———— 3. I take things or situations apart to find out how they work.

———— 4. I welcome uncertainty and unusual circumstances related to my tasks.

———— 5. I negotiate my salary openly with my supervisor.

———— 6. I can be counted on to find a new use for existing methods or equipment.

———— 7. Among my colleagues and co-workers, I will be the first or nearly the first to try out a new idea or method.

———— 8. I take the opportunity to translate communications from other departments for my work group.

———— 9. I demonstrate originality.

———— 10. I will work on a problem that has caused others great difficulty.

———— 11. I provide critical input toward a new solution.

———— 12. I provide written evaluations of proposed ideas.

———— 13. I develop contacts with experts outside my firm.

———— 14. I use personal contacts to maneuver myself into choice work assignments.

———— 15. I make time to pursue my own pet ideas or projects.

———— 16. I set aside resources for the pursuit of a risky project.

———— 17. I tolerate people who depart from organizational routine.

———— 18. I speak out in staff meetings.

———— 19. I work in teams to try to solve complex problems.

———— 20. If my co-workers are asked, they will say I am a wit.

SOURCE: Ettlie & O'Keefe (1982).

SKILL LEARNING

PROBLEM SOLVING, CREATIVITY, AND INNOVATION

Problem solving is a skill that is required of every person in almost every aspect of life. Seldom does an hour go by without an individual's being faced with the need to solve some kind of problem. The job of the manager is inherently a problem-solving job. If there were no problems in organizations, there would be no need for managers. Therefore, it is hard to conceive of an incompetent problem-solver succeeding as a manager.

In this module we offer specific guidelines and techniques for improving problem-solving skills. Two kinds of problem solving are addressed—rational problem solving and creative problem solving. Effective managers are able to solve problems both rationally and creatively, even though different kinds of skills are required for each type of problem. Rational problem solving is discussed first. It is the kind of problem solving that managers use frequently, many times each day. We then discuss creative problem solving, which occurs less frequently. Creative problem-solving ability, however, separates the heros from the goats, career successes from career failures, achievers from derailed executives, and can produce a dramatic impact on organizational effectiveness. The module concludes with a brief discussion of some ways in which effective managers can foster creative problem solving and innovation among people with whom they work.

STEPS IN RATIONAL PROBLEM SOLVING

Most people, including most managers, don't particularly like problems—they're time consuming, they create stress, and they never seem to go away. In fact, most people try to get rid of problems as soon as they can. Their natural tendency is to select the first reasonable solution that comes to mind (March & Simon, 1958). Unfortunately, that first solution is not often the best one. In normal problem solving, most people implement the marginally acceptable or merely satisfactory solution instead of the optimal or ideal solution. In fact, many observers have attributed primarily to the abandonment of correct problem-solving principles the decline in U.S. quality and competitiveness. Short cuts, they argue, have had a major negative effect on the American economy.

Defining the Problem

The most widely accepted model of **rational problem solving** involves four steps, which are summarized in Table 1. The first step is to define the problem. This involves diagnosing the situation so that the focus is on the real problem, not just on its symptoms. For example, suppose you must deal with the problem of an employee who consistently fails to get his or her work done on time. Slow work might be the problem, or it might be only a symptom of another underlying problem—bad health, low morale, lack of training, or inadequate rewards. Defining the problem, therefore, requires a wide search for information. The more information that is acquired, the more likely it is that the problem will be defined accurately. As Charles Kettering put it, "It ain't the things you don't know that'll get you in trouble, but the things you know for sure that ain't so."

The following are among the attributes of good problem definition:

1. Factual information is differentiated from opinion or speculation. (Objective data are separated from perceptions and suppositions.)

Table 1 A Model of Problem Solving

STEP	CHARACTERISTICS
1. Define the problem.	▪ Differentiate fact from opinion.
	▪ Specify underlying causes.
	▪ Tap everyone involved for information.
	▪ State the problem explicitly.
	▪ Identify what standard is violated.
	▪ Determine whose problem it is.
	▪ Avoid stating the problem as a disguised solution.
2. Generate alternative solutions.	▪ Postpone evaluating alternatives.
	▪ Be sure all involved individuals generate alternatives.
	▪ Specify alternatives that are consistent with goals.
	▪ Specify both short-term and long-term alternatives.
	▪ Build on others' ideas.
	▪ Specify alternatives that solve the problem.
3. Evaluate and select an alternative.	▪ Evaluate relative to an optimal standard.
	▪ Evaluate systematically.
	▪ Evaluate relative to goals.
	▪ Evaluate main effects and side effects.
	▪ State the selected alternative explicitly.
4. Implement and follow up on the solution.	▪ Implement at the proper time and in the right sequence.
	▪ Provide opportunities for feedback.
	▪ Engender acceptance of those who are affected.
	▪ Establish an ongoing monitoring system.
	▪ Evaluate based on problem solution.

2. All individuals involved are tapped as information sources. (Broad participation is encouraged.)

3. The problem is stated explicitly. (Stating the problem specifically often helps point out ambiguities in the definition.)

4. The problem definition identifies what standard or expectation has been violated. (Problems always violate some standard or expectation; otherwise, they are not problems. Be clear about what the standard or expectation is.)

5. The problem definition indicates whose problem it is. (No problems are completely independent of people. It is a problem for someone.)

6. The definition is not simply a disguised solution. ("The problem is that we need to fire the slow employee" is inappropriate because the problem is stated as a solution.)

Managers often propose problem solutions before an adequate definition of the problem has been given, and this may lead to solving the wrong problem. The definition step in problem solving, therefore, is extremely important.

Generating Alternatives

The second step is to generate alternative solutions. This requires postponing the selection of one solution until several alternatives have been proposed. Maier (1970) has found that the quality of the final problem solution can be significantly enhanced by considering multiple alternatives. Judgment and evaluation, therefore, must be postponed so the first acceptable solution suggested isn't the one that is immediately selected. As Broadwell (1972, p. 121) noted:

> The problem with evaluating [an alternative] too early is that we may rule out some good ideas by just not getting around to thinking about them. We hit on an idea that sounds good and we go with it, thereby never even thinking of alternatives that may be better in the long run.

Many alternative solutions should be generated before evaluating any of them. A common problem in managerial decision making is that alternatives are evaluated as they are proposed, so the first acceptable (although frequently not optimal) one is chosen.

Some attributes of good alternative generation are the following:

1. The evaluation of each proposed alternative is postponed. (All alternatives should be proposed before evaluation is allowed.)

2. Alternatives are proposed by all individuals involved in the problem. (Broad participation in alternative proposals improves solution quality and group acceptance.)

3. Alternative solutions are consistent with organizational goals or policies. (Subversion and criticism are detrimental to both the organization and the alternative generation process.)

4. Alternatives take into consideration both the short-term and the long-term consequences.

5. Alternatives build on one another. (Bad ideas may become good ideas if combined with or modified by other ideas.)

6. Alternatives solve the problem that has been defined. (Another problem may also be important, but it should be ignored if it does not directly affect the problem being considered.)

Evaluating Alternatives

The third problem-solving step is to evaluate and select an alternative. This step involves careful weighing of the advantages and disadvantages of the proposed alternatives before making a final selection. In selecting the best alternative, skilled problem solvers make sure that the alternatives are judged in terms of: the extent to which they will solve the problem without causing other unanticipated problems; the extent to which all the individuals involved will accept the alternative; the extent to which implementation of the alternative is likely; and the extent to which the alternative fits within the organizational constraints (e.g., is consistent with policies, norms, and budget limitations). Care is taken not to short-circuit these considerations by choosing the most conspicuous alternative without considering others. As March and Simon (1958, p. 141) point out:

> Most human decision making, whether individual or organizational, is concerned with the discovery and selection of satisfactory alternatives ... ly in exceptional ca⸳ ... imal
> alternatives. ... e more
> complex tha⸳ ... etween
> searching a h ...
> haystack to f ...

Given the n ... proposed,
this step deserve ...
Some attribu ...

1. Alternatives ... than a
   satisfactory s ...

2. Evaluation o ... onsideration. (Short- ... ter-
   natives.)

3. Alternatives ⸳ ... n and
   the individua ... ile individual prefe ...

4. Alternatives a ... of their probable effects. (Both side effects and direct effects on the problem are considered.)

5. The alternative selected is stated explicitly. (Specifying the alternative can help uncover latent ambiguities and let others know about the solution selected.)

Implementing the Solution

The final step is to implement and follow up on the solution. Implementation of any solution requires sensitivity to possible resistance from those who will be affected by it. Almost any change engenders some resistance. Therefore, the best problem solvers are careful to select a strategy that maximizes the probability that the solution will be accepted and fully implemented. This may involve ordering that the solution be implemented by others, "selling" the solution to others, or involving others in the implementation. Tannenbaum and Schmidt (1958) and Vroom and Yetton (1973) provide guidelines for managers to determine which of these implementation behaviors is most appropriate under which circumstances. Generally speaking, participation by others in the implementation of a solution will increase its acceptance and decrease resistance.

Effective implementation also requires some followup to check on implementation, prevent negative side-effects, and ensure solution of the problem. Followup not only helps ensure effective implementation but serves a feedback function as well by providing information that can be used to improve future problem solving. Drucker (1974, p. 480) explained:

> A feedback has to be built into the decision to provide continuous testing, against actual events, of the expectations that underlie the decision. Few decisions work out the way they are intended to. Even the best decision usually runs into snags, unexpected obstacles, and all kinds of surprises. Even the most effective decision eventually becomes obsolete. Unless there is feedback from the results of the decision, it is unlikely to produce the desired results.

Some attributes of effective implementation and followup are these:

1. Implementation occurs at the right time and in the proper sequence. (It does not ignore constraining factors, and it does not come before steps 1, 2, and 3 in the problem-solving process.)

2. The implementation process includes opportunities for feedback. (How well the selected solution works needs to be communicated.)

3. Implementation engenders support and acceptance by those affected by it. (Participation is often the best way to ensure acceptance by others.)

4. An ongoing monitoring system is set up for the implemented solution. (Long-term as well as short-term effects should be assessed.)

5. Evaluation of success is based on problem solution, not on side benefits. (Although the solution may provide some positive outcomes, unless it solves the problem being considered, it is unsuccessful.)

LIMITATIONS OF THE RATIONAL PROBLEM-SOLVING MODEL

Most experienced problem solvers are familiar with these steps in rational problem solving, which are based on empirical research results and sound rationale (Maier, 1970; Huber, 1980; Elbing, 1978; Filley, House, & Kerr, 1976). Unfortunately, managers do not always practice them. The demands of the job often pressure managers into circumventing some of these steps, and problem solving suffers as a result. When these four steps are followed, however, effective problem solving is markedly enhanced.

On the other hand, simply learning about and practicing these four steps do not guarantee that an individual will effectively solve all types of problems. There are two reasons: First, these problem-solving steps are useful mainly when the problems faced are straightforward, when alternatives are readily available, when relevant information is present, and when a clear standard exists against which to judge the correctness of a solution. Thompson and Tuden (1959) call problems with these characteristics "computational problems," for which the main tasks are to gather information, generate alternatives, and make an informed choice. The trouble is, many managerial problems are not of this type. Definitions, information, alternatives, and standards are seldom unambiguous or readily available, so knowing the steps in problem solving and being able to implement them are not the same thing.

Table 2 summarizes some of the reasons why rational problem solving is not always effective in the day-to-day situations managers face. Constraints exist on each of these four steps. These constraints, for the most part, are products of other individuals or of organizational processes that make it difficult to follow the prescribed model.

A second reason why the rational problem-solving model is not always effective for managers is because of the nature of the problem itself. The problem may not be amenable to a systematic or rational analysis. In fact, for some problems, a rational problem-solving approach may not lead to an effective solution. Sufficient and accurate information may not be available, outcomes may not

Table 2 Some Constraints on the Rational Problem-Solving Model

STEPS	CONSTRAINTS
1. Define the problem.	■ There is seldom consensus as to the definition of the problem.
	■ There is often uncertainty as to whose definition will be accepted.
	■ Problems are usually defined in terms of the solutions already possessed.
2. Generate alternative solutions.	■ Solution alternatives are usually evaluated one at a time as they are proposed.
	■ Few of the possible alternatives are usually known.
	■ The first acceptable solution is usually accepted.
	■ Alternatives are based on what was successful in the past.
3. Evaluate and select an alternative.	■ Limited information about each alternative is usually available.
	■ Search for information occurs close to home—in easily accessible places.
	■ The type of information available is constrained by factors such as primacy versus recency, extremity versus centrality, expected versus surprising, and correlation versus causation.
	■ Gathering information on each alternative is costly.
	■ Preferences of which is the best alternative are not always known.
	■ Satisfactory solutions, not optimal ones, are usually accepted.
	■ Solutions are often selected by oversight or default.
	■ Solutions often are implemented before the problem is defined.
4. Implement and follow up on the solution.	■ Acceptance by others of the solution is not always forthcoming.
	■ Resistance to change is a universal phenomenon.
	■ It is not always clear what part of the solution should be monitored or measured in follow-up.
	■ Political and organizational processes must be managed in any implementation effort.
	■ It may take a long time to implement a solution.

be predictable, or means-ends connections may not be evident. In order to solve such problems, a new way of thinking may be required, multiple or conflicting definitions might be needed, alternatives never before considered may have to be generated; in short, creative problem solving must be used.

IMPEDIMENTS TO CREATIVE PROBLEM SOLVING

Most people have trouble solving problems creatively. They have developed certain conceptual blocks in their problem-solving activities that they are not even aware of. These blocks inhibit them from solving certain problems effectively. These blocks are largely personal, as opposed to interpersonal or organizational, so skill development is required to overcome them. **Conceptual blocks** are mental obstacles that constrain the way the problem is defined and limit the number of alternative solutions thought to be relevant (Allen, 1974). Every individual has conceptual blocks, but they are more numerous and more intense in some people than in others. These blocks are largely unrecognized or unconscious, so the only way individuals can be made aware of them is to be confronted with problems that are unsolvable because of them. Conceptual blocks result largely from individual thinking processes and to the ways problem solvers use their minds when facing problems. Everyone develops some conceptual blocks over time. They need them to cope with everyday life. Here's why.

At every moment, each of us is bombarded with far more information than we can possibly pay attention to. For example, you are probably not conscious right now of the temperature of the room, the color of your skin, the level of illumination overhead, or how your toes feel in your shoes. Yet all of this information is available to you and is being processed by your brain. It is just that you have tuned out some things and focused on other things. Over time, you must develop the habit of mentally filtering out some of the information you are exposed to; otherwise, information overload would drive you crazy. These filtering habits eventually become conceptual blocks. Though you are not conscious of these blocks, they actually inhibit you from registering some kinds of information and, therefore, from solving certain kinds of problems.

Paradoxically, the more formal education individuals have, the more experience they have in a job, the less able they are to solve problems in creative ways. It has been estimated that most adults over forty display less than 2 percent of the creative problem-solving ability of a child under five. That's because formal education often produces "right answers," analytic rules, or thinking boundaries. Experience in a job teaches proper ways of doing things, specialized knowledge, and rigid expectation of appropriate actions. Individuals lose the ability to experiment, improvise, or take mental detours. Consider the following example:

> If you place in a bottle half a dozen bees and the same number of flies, and lay the bottle down horizontally, with its base to the window, you will find that the bees will persist, till they die of exhaustion or hunger, in their endeavor to discover an issue through the glass; while the flies, in less than two minutes, will all have sallied forth through the neck on the opposite

side. . . . It is [the bees'] love of light, it is their very intelligence, that is their undoing in this experiment. They evidently imagine that the issue from every prison must be there when the light shines clearest; and they act in accordance, and persist in too logical an action. To them glass is a supernatural mystery they never have met in nature; they have had no experience of this suddenly impenetrable atmosphere; and the greater their intelligence, the more inadmissible, more incomprehensible, will the strange obstacle appear. Whereas the feather-brained flies, careless of logic as of the enigma of crystal, disregarding the call of the light, flutter wildly, hither and thither, meeting here the good fortune that often waits on the simple, who find salvation there where the wiser will perish, necessarily end by discovering the friendly opening that restores their liberty to them (Sill, 1968, p. 189).

This illustration identifies a paradox inherent in learning to solve problems creatively. On the one hand, more education and experience may inhibit creative problem solving and reinforce conceptual blocks. As bees, individuals may not find solutions because the problem requires less "educated" or more seemingly playful approaches. On the other hand, as several researchers have found, training directed toward improving thinking significantly enhances creative problem-solving abilities and managerial effectiveness (Barron, 1963; Taylor & Barron, 1963; Torrance, 1965).

Parnes (1962), for example, found that training in thinking increased the number of good ideas produced in problem solving by 125 percent. Bower (1965) recorded numerous examples of organizations that increased profitability and efficiency through training in the improvement of thinking skills. Many name-brand organizations such as IBM, General Electric, and AT&T now send their executives to creativity workshops in order to improve their creative-thinking abilities. Creative problem-solving consultants are currently hot property on the consulting circuit. And about a million books on creativity are sold each year in this country. Several well-known products have been produced as a direct result of this kind of training, for example, NASA's Velcro snaps, G.E.'s self-diagnostic dishwashers, Mead's carbonless copy paper, and Kodak's Trimprint film.

A resolution to this paradox is not just more exposure to information or education; it is rather to focus on the *process* of thinking about certain problems in a creative way. As John Gardner (1965, p. 21) stated, it is learning to *use* the mind rather than merely *filling up* the mind.

All too often we are giving our young people cut flowers when we should be teaching them to grow plants. We are stuffing their heads with the products of earlier innovation rather than teaching them to innovate. We think of the mind as a storehouse to be filled when we should be thinking of it as an instrument to be used.

In the next section, we focus on problems that require creative rather than rational solutions. These are problems for which no acceptable alternative seems to be available, all reasonable solutions seem to be blocked, or no obvious best answer is accessible. This situation exists because conceptual blocks inhibit the implementation of rational problem solving. Our focus, therefore, must be on tools and techniques that help overcome conceptual blocks and unlock problem-solving creativity.

Two examples help illustrate the kinds of problems that require creative problem-solving skill. They illustrate several conceptual blocks that inhibit problem solving and several techniques and tools that can be used to overcome them. We will refer to these examples several times in the remainder of the module.

Percy Spencer's Magnetron

During World War II, the British developed one of the best-kept military secrets of the war—a special radar detector based on a device called the magnetron. This radar was credited with turning the tide of battle in the war between Britain and Germany and helping the British withstand Hitler's *Blitzkrieg*. In 1940, Raytheon was one of several U.S. firms invited to produce magnetrons for the war effort.

The workings of a magnetron were not well understood, even by sophisticated physicists. Even among the firms that made them, few understood what made the device work. A magnetron was tested, in those early days, by holding a neon tube next to it. If the neon tube got bright enough, the magnetron tube passed the test. In the process of conducting the test, the hands of the scientist holding the neon tube got warm. It was this phenomenon that led to a major creative breakthrough that eventually transformed lifestyles throughout the world.

At the end of the war, the market for radar essentially dried up, and most firms stopped producing magnetrons. In Raytheon, however, a scientist named Percy Spencer had been fooling around with magnetrons, trying to think of alternative uses for the devices. He was convinced that magnetrons could be used to cook food by using the heat produced in the neon tube for food preparation. The problem was, Raytheon was in the defense business. Next to its two prize products—the Hawk and the Sparrow missiles—cooking devices seemed odd and out of place. Percy Spencer was convinced that Raytheon should continue to produce magnetrons, even though production costs were prohibitively high. But Raytheon had lost money on the devices, and now there was no available market for magnetrons. The consumer product Spencer had in mind did not fit within the bounds of Raytheon's business.

As it turned out, Percy Spencer's solution to Raytheon's problem produced the microwave oven and a revolution in the cooking methods of the middle class throughout the entire world. Further on, we will analyze several of the problem-solving techniques that are illustrated by his creative triumph.

Spence Silver's Glue

A second example of creative problem solving began with Spence Silver's assignment to work on a temporary project team within the 3M company. The team was searching for new adhesives, so Silver obtained some material from AMD, Inc., which had potential for a new polymer-based adhesive. He described one of his experiments in this way: "In the course of this exploration, I tried an experiment with one of the monomers in which I wanted to see what would happen if I put a lot of it into the reaction mixture. Before, we had used amounts that would correspond to conventional wisdom" (Nayak & Ketteringham, 1986). The result was a substance that failed all the conventional 3M tests for adhesives. It didn't stick. It preferred its own molecules to the molecules of any other substance. It was more cohesive than adhesive. It sort of "hung around without making a commitment." It was a "now-it-works, now-it-doesn't" kind of glue.

For five years Silver went from department to department within the company trying to find someone interested in using his newly found substance in a product. Silver had found a solution; he just couldn't find a problem to solve with it. Predictably, 3M showed little interest. The company's mission was to make adhesives that adhered ever more tightly. The ultimate adhesive was one that formed an unbreakable bond, not one that formed a temporary bond.

After four years the task force was disbanded, and team members were assigned to other projects. But Silver was still convinced that his substance was good for something. He just didn't know what. As it turned out, Silver's solution has become the prototype for innovation in American firms, and it has spawned a half-billion dollars in annual revenues for 3M—in a unique product called Post-It Notes.

These two examples are positive illustrations of how solving a problem in a unique way can lead to phenomenal business success. Creative problem solving can have remarkable effects on both individuals' careers and on business success. To understand how to solve problems creatively, however, we must first reveal the blocks that inhibit this approach.

CONCEPTUAL BLOCKS

Table 3 summarizes four types of conceptual blocks that inhibit creative problem solving. Each is discussed and illustrated below with problems or exercises. We

Table 3 Conceptual Blocks That Inhibit Creative Problem Solving

1. CONSTANCY	
Vertical thinking	Defining a problem in only one way without considering alternative views.
One thinking language	Not using more than one language to define and assess the problem.
2. COMMITMENT	
Stereotyping based on past experience	Present problems are seen only as the variations of past problems.
Ignoring commonalities	Failing to perceive commonalities among elements that initially appear to be different.
3. COMPRESSION	
Distinguishing figure from ground	Not filtering out irrelevant information or finding needed information.
Artificial constraints	Defining the boundaries of a problem too narrowly.
4. COMPLACENCY	
Noninquisitiveness	Not asking questions.
Non thinking	A bias toward activity in place of mental work.

encourage you to complete the exercises and to solve the problems as you read the module because doing so will help you become aware of your own conceptual blocks. Later we shall discuss in more detail how you can overcome them.

Constancy

Constancy means that an individual becomes wedded to one way of looking at a problem or to using one approach to define, describe, or solve it. It is easy to see why constancy is common in problem solving since being constant, or consistent, is a highly valued attribute for most of us. We like to appear at least moderately consistent in our approach to life, and constancy is often associated with maturity, honesty, and even intelligence. We judge lack of constancy as untrustworthy, peculiar, or airheaded. Several prominent psychologists theorize, in fact, that a need for constancy is the primary motivator of human behavior (Festinger, 1957; Heider, 1946; Newcomb, 1954). Many psychological studies have shown that once individuals take a stand or employ a particular approach to a problem, they are highly likely to pursue that same course without deviation in the future (see Cialdini, 1988, for multiple examples).

On the other hand, constancy can inhibit solution of some kinds of problems. Consistency sometimes drives out creativity. Two illustrations of the constancy block are *vertical thinking* and using only one *thinking language*.

Vertical Thinking

The term **vertical thinking** was coined by Edward deBono (1968). It refers to defining a problem in a single way, then pursuing that definition without deviation until a solution is reached. No alternative definitions are considered. All information gathered and all alternatives generated are consistent with the original definition. In a search for oil, for example, vertical thinkers determine a spot for the hole and drill the hole deeper and deeper until they strike oil. Lateral thinkers, on the other hand, generate alternative ways of viewing a problem and produce multiple definitions. Instead of drilling one hole deeper and deeper, lateral thinkers drill a number of holes in different places in search of oil. The vertical-thinking conceptual block arises from not being able to view the problem from multiple perspectives—to drill several holes—or to think laterally as well as vertically in problem solving. Problem definition is restricted.

Plenty of examples exist of creative solutions that have occurred because an individual refused to get stuck with a single problem definition. Alexander Graham Bell was trying to devise a hearing aid when he shifted definitions and invented the telephone. Colonel Sanders was trying to sell his recipe to restaurants when he shifted definitions and developed his Kentucky Fried Chicken business. Karl Jansky was studying telephone static when he shifted definitions, discovered radio waves from the Milky Way galaxy, and developed the science of radio astronomy.

In the development of the microwave industry described earlier, Percy Spencer shifted the definition of the problem from "How can we save our military radar business at the end of the war?" to "What other applications can be made for the magnetron?" Other problem definitions followed, such as "How can we make magnetrons cheaper?" "How can we mass-produce magnetrons?" "How can we convince someone besides the military to buy magnetrons?" "How can we enter a consumer products market?" "How can we make microwave ovens practical and safe?" And so on. Each new problem definition led to new ways of thinking about the problem, new alternative approaches, and, eventually, to a new microwave oven industry.

Spence Silver at 3M is, likewise, an example of someone who changed problem definitions. He began with "How can I get an adhesive that has a stronger bond?" but switched to "How can I find an application for an adhesive that doesn't stick?" Eventually, other problem definitions followed such as, "How can we get this new glue to stick to one surface but not another (e.g., to notepaper but not normal paper)?" "How can we replace staples, thumbtacks, and paperclips in the workplace?" "How can we manufacture and package a product that uses nonadhesive glue?" "How can we get anyone to pay $1.00 a pad for scratch paper?" And so on.

Shifting definitions is not easy, of course, because it is not natural. It requires that individuals deflect their tendencies toward constancy. We will discuss some hints and tools later that can help overcome the constancy block while avoiding the negative consequences of being inconsistent.

A Single Thinking Language

A second manifestation of the constancy block is the use of only one thinking language. Most people think in words—that is, they think about a problem and its solution in terms of verbal language. Rational problem solving reinforces this approach. Some writers, in fact, have argued that thinking cannot even occur without words (Vygotsky, 1962). Other thought languages are available, however, such as nonverbal or symbolic languages (e.g., mathematics), sensory imagery (e.g., smelling or tactile sensation), feelings and emotions (e.g., happiness, fear, or anger), and visual imagery (e.g., mental pictures). The more languages available to problem solvers, the better and more creative will be their solutions. As Koestler (1967) puts it, "[Verbal] language can become a screen which stands between the thinker and reality. This is the reason that true creativity often starts where [verbal] language ends."

Percy Spencer at Raytheon is a prime example of a visual thinker:

One day, while Spencer was lunching with Dr. Ivan Getting and several other Raytheon scientists, a mathematical question arose. Several men, in a familiar reflex, pulled out their slide rules, but before any could complete the equation, Spencer gave the answer. Dr. Getting was astonished. "How did you do that?" he asked. "The root," said Spencer shortly. "I learned cube roots and squares by using blocks as a boy. Since then, all I have to do is visualize them placed together." (Scott, 1974, p. 287).

The microwave oven not only depended on Spencer's command of multiple thinking languages, but it would never have gotten off the ground without a critical incident that illustrates the power of visual thinking. By 1965, Raytheon was just about to give up on any consumer application of the magnetron when a meeting was held with George Foerstner, the president of the recently acquired Amana

Refrigeration Company. In the meeting, costs, applications, manufacturing obstacles, and so on were discussed. Foerstner galvanized the entire microwave oven effort with the following statement, as reported by a Raytheon vice president.

> George says, "It's no problem. It's about the same size as an air conditioner. It weighs about the same. It should sell for the same. So we'll price it at $499." Now you think that's silly, but you stop and think about it. Here's a man who really didn't understand the technologies. But there is about the same amount of copper involved, the same amount of steel as an air conditioner. And these are basic raw materials. It didn't make a lot of difference how you fit them together to make them work. They're both boxes; they're both made out of sheet metal; and they both require some sort of trim. (Nayak & Ketteringham, 1986, p. 181).

In several short sentences Foerstner had taken one of the most complicated military secrets of World War II and translated it into something no more complex than a room air conditioner. He had painted a picture of an application that no one else had been able to capture by describing a magnetron visually, as a familiar object, not as a set of calculations, formulas, or blueprints.

A similar occurrence in the Post-It Note chronology also led to a breakthrough. Spence Silver had been trying for years to get someone in 3M to adopt his un-sticky glue. Art Fry, another scientist with 3M, had heard Silver's presentations before. One day while singing in North Presbyterian Church in St. Paul, Minnesota, Fry was fumbling around with the slips of paper that marked the various hymns in his book. Suddenly, a visual image popped into his mind.

> "I thought, Gee, if I had a little adhesive on these bookmarks, that would be just the ticket. So I decided to check into that idea the next week at work. What I had in mind was Silver's adhesive. . . . I knew I had a much bigger discovery than that. I also now realized that the primary application for Silver's adhesive was not to put it on a fixed surface like the bulletin boards. That was a secondary application. The primary application concerned paper to paper. I realized that immediately" (Nayak & Ketteringham, 1986, p. 63–64).

Years of verbal descriptions had not led to any application for Silver's glue. Tactile thinking (handling the glue) also had not produced many ideas. However, thinking about the product in visual terms, as applied to what Fry initially called "a better bookmark," led to the breakthrough that was needed.

This emphasis on using alternative thinking languages, especially visual thinking, is now becoming the new frontier in scientific research. With the advent of supercomputers, scientists are more and more working with pictures and simulated images rather than with numerical data. "Scientists who are using the new computer graphics say that by viewing images instead of numbers, a fundamental change in the way researchers think and work is occurring. People have a lot easier time getting an intuition from pictures than they do from numbers and tables or formulas. In most physics experiments, the answer used to be a number or a string of numbers. In the last few years the answer has increasingly become a picture" (Markoff, 1988, p. D3).

To illustrate the differences among thinking languages, consider the following two simple problems.

1. Below is the Roman numeral 9. By adding only a *single* line, turn it into a 6.

IX

2. Figure 1 shows seven matchsticks. By moving only *one* matchstick, make the figure into a true equality (i.e., the value on one side equals the value on the other side). Before looking up the answers in Appendix I, page 89, try defining the problems differently, and try using different thinking languages. How many answers can you find?

Commitment

Commitment can also serve as a conceptual block to creative problem solving. Once individuals become committed to a particular point of view, definition, or solution, it is likely that they will follow through on that commitment. Freedman and Fraser (1966), for example, found that only 17 percent of a sample of Californians agreed to have a large, poorly lettered DRIVE CAREFULLY sign placed on their front lawn. However, in another study, another group of Californians were asked to sign a petition favoring "keeping California beautiful." Two weeks later, a full 76 percent of them were then willing to put up the DRIVE CAREFULLY sign. By signing a petition, they had become committed to the idea that they were responsible citizens. The large, unsightly sign became the visible evidence of their commitment.

A host of other studies have demonstrated the same phenomenon—that commitment can sometimes lead to dysfunctional or foolish decisions, rigidly defended. Two forms of commitment that produce conceptual blocks are *stereotyping based on past experiences* and *ignoring commonalities*.

Stereotyping Based on Past Experiences

March and Simon (1958) point out that a major obstacle to innovative problem solving is that individuals tend to define present problems in terms of problems they have faced in the past. Current problems are usually seen as variations on some past situation, so the alternatives proposed to solve the current problem are ones

Figure 1

The Matchstick
Configuration

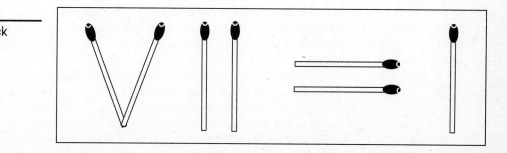

that have proven successful in the past. Both problem definition and proposed solution are therefore restricted by past experience. This restriction is referred to as **perceptual stereotyping** (Allen, 1974). That is, certain preconceptions formed on the basis of past experience determine how an individual defines a situation.

In other words, when individuals receive an initial cue regarding the definition of a problem, all subsequent problems frequently are framed in terms of the initial cue. Of course, this is not all bad, because perceptual stereotyping helps organize problems on the basis of a limited amount of data, and the need to consciously analyze every problem encountered is eliminated. On the other hand, perceptual stereotyping prevents individuals from viewing a problem in novel ways.

Both the creation of microwave ovens and that of Post-It Notes provide examples of overcoming stereotyping based on past experiences. Scott (1974) described the first meeting of John D. Cockcroft, the technical leader of the British radar system that invented magnetrons, and Percy Spencer of Raytheon.

> Cockcroft liked Spencer at once. He showed him the magnetron, and the American regarded it thoughtfully. He asked questions—very intelligent ones—about how it was produced, and the Britisher answered at length. Later Spencer wrote, "The technique of making these tubes, as described to us, was awkward and impractical." *Awkward and impractical!* Nobody else dared draw such a judgment about a product of undoubted scientific brilliance, produced and displayed by the leaders of British science.

Despite his admiration for Cockcroft and the magnificent magnetron, Spencer refused to abandon his curious and inquisitive stance. Rather than adopting the stance of other scientists and assume that since the British invented it and were using it, they surely knew how to produce a magnetron, Spencer broke out of the stereotypes and pushed for improvements.

Similarly, Spence Silver at 3M described his invention in terms of breaking stereotypes based on past experience.

> The key to the Post-It adhesive was doing the experiment. If I had sat down and factored it out beforehand, and thought about it, I wouldn't have done the experiment. If I had really seriously cracked the books and gone through the literature, I would have stopped. The literature was full of examples that said you can't do this (Nayak & Ketteringham, 1986, p. 57).

This is not to say that one should avoid learning from past experience or that failing to learn the mistakes of history does not doom us to repeat them. Rather, it is to say that commitment to a course of action based on past experience can sometimes inhibit viewing problems in new ways, and it can even inhibit us from being able to solve some problems at all. Consider the following problem as an example.

There are four volumes of Shakespeare on the shelf (see Figure 2). The pages of each volume are exactly two inches thick. The covers are each one-sixth of an inch thick. A bookworm started eating at page 1 of Volume 1 and ate straight through to the last page of Volume IV. What is the distance the worm covered? (See Appendix I, page 89, for the answer.) Solving this problem is relatively simple, but it requires that you overcome a stereotyping block to get the correct answer.

Figure 2

Shakespeare Riddle

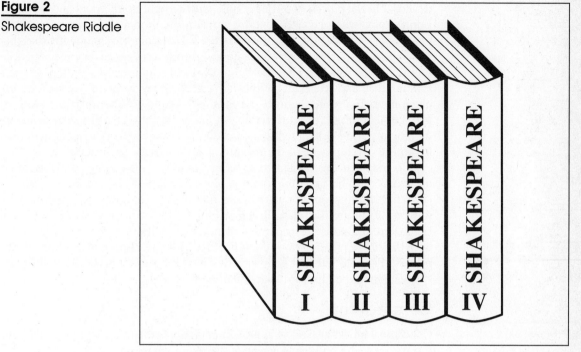

SOURCE: Raudsepp & Hough, 1977.

Ignoring Commonalities

A second manifestation of the commitment block is failure to identify similarities among seemingly disparate pieces of data. This is among the most commonly identified blocks to creativity. It means that a person becomes committed to a particular point of view, to the fact that elements are different, and becomes unable to make connections, identify themes, or to perceive commonalities.

The ability to find one definition or solution for two seemingly dissimilar problems is a characteristic of creative individuals (Dellas & Gaier, 1970; Steiner, 1978). The inability to do this can overload a problem solver by requiring that every problem encountered be solved individually. The discovery of penicillin by Sir Alexander Fleming resulted from his seeing a common theme among seemingly unrelated events. Fleming was working with some cultures of staphylococci that had accidentally become contaminated. The contamination, a growth of fungi, and isolated clusters of dead staphylococci led Fleming to see a relationship no one else had ever seen previously and thus to discover a wonder drug (Beveridge, 1960). The famous chemist Friedrich Kekule saw a relationship between his dream of a snake swallowing its own tail and the chemical structure of organic compounds. This creative insight led him to the discovery that organic compounds such as benzene have closed rings rather than open structures (Koestler, 1967).

For Percy Spencer at Raytheon, seeing a connection between the heat of a neon tube and the heat required to cook food was the creative connection that led to his breakthrough in the microwave industry. One of Spencer's colleagues recalled: "In the process of testing a bulb [with a magnetron], your hands got hot. I don't know when Percy really came up with the thought of microwave ovens, but he knew at that time—and that was 1942. He [remarked] frequently that this would be a good device for cooking food." Another colleague described Spencer this way: "The way Percy Spencer's mind worked is an interesting thing. He had a mind that allowed him to hold an extraordinary array of associations on phenomena and relate them to one another." (Nayak & Ketteringham, 1986, p. 184, 205). Similarly, the connection Art Fry made between a glue that wouldn't stick tightly and marking hymns in a choir book was the final breakthrough that led to the development of the revolutionary Post-It Note business.

To test your own ability to see commonalities, answer the following three questions: (1) What are some common terms that apply to both *water* and *finance?* (2) What is humorous about the following story: "Descartes, the philosopher, walked into a university class. Recognizing him, the instructor asked if he would like to lecture. Descartes replied, 'I think not,' and promptly disappeared." (3) What does the single piece of wood look like that will pass through each hole in the block in Figure 3 but that will perfectly fill each hole as it passes through? (Answers are in Appendix I on pages 89 and 90.)

Compression

Conceptual blocks also occur as a result of compression of ideas—that is, looking too narrowly at a problem, screening out too much relevant data, or making assumptions that inhibit problem solution are common examples. Two especially cogent examples of compression are *artificially constraining problems* and *not distinguishing figure from ground*.

Figure 3 A Block Problem

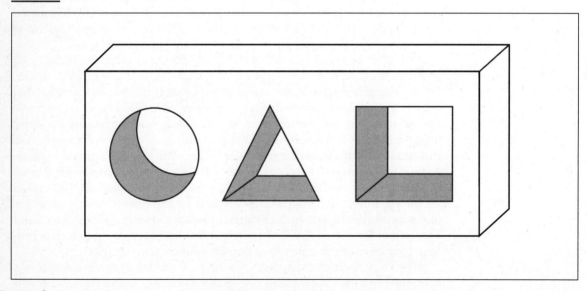

SOURCE: McKim, 1972.

Figure 4

The Nine-Dot
Problem

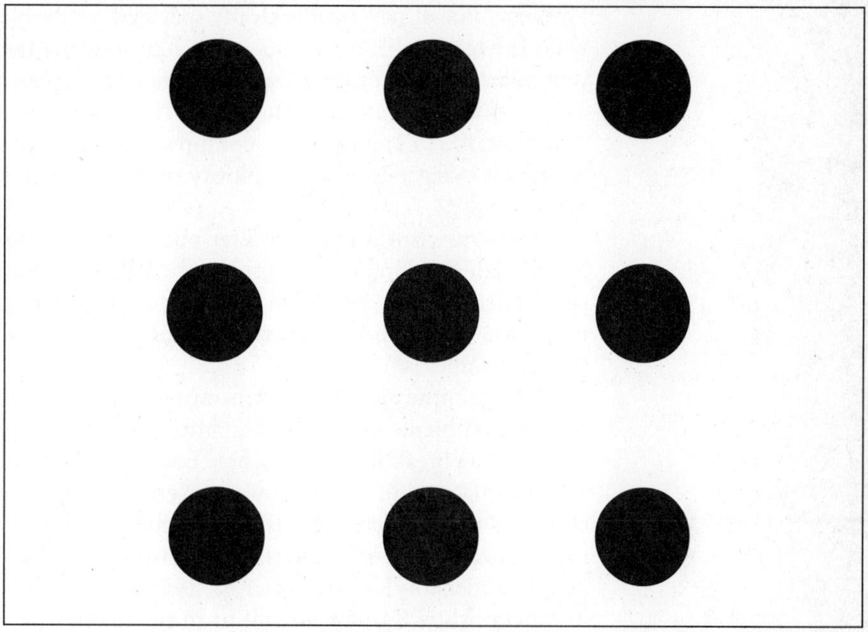

Artificial Constraints

Sometimes people place boundaries around problems, or constrain their approach to them, in such a way that the problems become impossible to solve. Such constraints arise from hidden assumptions people make about problems they encounter. People assume that some problem definitions or alternative solutions are off-limits, and so they ignore them. For an illustration of this conceptual block, look at Figure 4. Without lifting your pencil from the paper, draw four straight lines that pass through all nine dots. Complete the task before reading further.

By thinking of the figure as more constrained than it actually is, the problem becomes impossible to solve. Try to break out of your own limiting assumptions on the problem. (One four-line answer is presented in Appendix I, page 90.) Now that you have been cued, can you do the same task with only three lines? Work on this problem for a minute. If you are successful, try to do the task with only one line. Can you determine how to put a single straight line through all nine dots without lifting your pencil from the paper? Both the three-line solution and some one-line solutions are in the Appendix.

Artificially constraining problems means simply that the problem definition and the possible alternatives are limited more than the problem requires. Creative problem solving requires that individuals become adept at recognizing their hidden assumptions and expanding the alternatives they consider. We shall consider ways to do that later.

Separating Figure from Ground

Another illustration of the compression block is the reverse of artificial constraints. It is the inability to sufficiently constrain problems so that they can be solved.

Problems almost never come clearly specified, so problem solvers must determine what the real problem is. They must filter out inaccurate, misleading, or irrelevant information in order to correctly define the problem and to generate appropriate alternative solutions. The inability to separate the important from the unimportant, to appropriately compress problems, serves as a conceptual block because it exaggerates the complexity of the problem and inhibits a simple definition.

How easy is it for you to filter out irrelevant information? Consider Figure 5. For each pair, find the pattern on the left that is embedded in the more complex pattern on the right. On the complex pattern, outline the embedded pattern. Now try to find at least two figures in each pattern. (See Appendix I, page 91, for a solution.)

This compression block—separating figure from ground and artificially constraining problems—also played an important role in the microwave oven and the Post-It Note breakthroughs. George Foerstner's contribution to the development and manufacture of the microwave oven was directly a product of his ability to compress the problem, that is, to separate out all the irrelevant complexity that constrained others. Whereas the magnetron was a device so complicated that few people understood it, Foerstner focused on its basic raw materials, its size, and its functionality. By comparing it to an air conditioner, he eliminated much of the complexity and mystery, and, as described by two analysts, "he had seen what all the researchers had failed to see, and they knew he was right" (Nayak & Ketteringham, 1986, p. 181).

On the other hand, Spence Silver had to *add* complexity, to *overcome* compression, in order to find an application for his product. Because the glue had failed every traditional 3M test for adhesives, it was categorized as a useless configuration of chemicals. The potential for the product was artificially constrained by traditional assumptions about adhesives—*more* stickiness, *stronger* bonding—until Art Fry visualized some unconventional applications—a better bookmark, a bulletin board, scratch paper, and, paradoxically, a replacement for 3M's main product, tape.

Complacency

Some conceptual blocks occur not because of poor thinking habits or because of inappropriate assumptions but because of fear, ignorance, insecurity, or just plain mental laziness. Two especially prevalent examples of the complacency block are a *lack of questioning* and *a bias against thinking*.

Noninquisitiveness

Sometimes the inability to solve problems results from a reticence to ask questions, to obtain information, or to search for data. Individuals might think that they will appear naive or ignorant if they question something or attempt to redefine a problem. Asking questions puts them at risk of exposing their ignorance. It also may be threatening to others because it implies that what they accept may not be correct. This may create resistance, conflict, or even ridicule by others.

Creative problem solving is inherently risky, therefore, because it potentially involves interpersonal conflict. In addition, it is also risky because it is fraught with mistakes. As Linus Pauling, the Nobel laureate, said, "If you want to have a good idea, have a lot of them, because most of them will be bad ones." Years of non-supportive socialization, however, blocks the adventuresome and inquisitive stance in most people. Most of us are not rewarded for bad ideas. To illustrate, answer the following questions for yourself.

Figure 5

Embedded Patterns

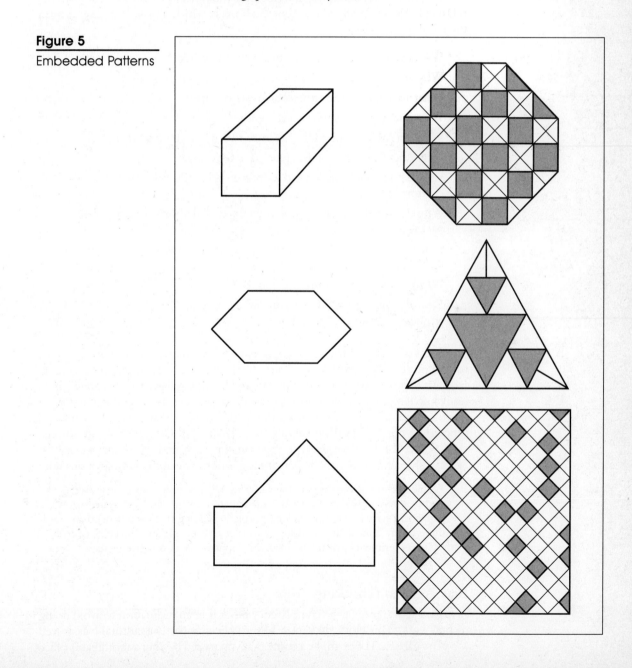

1. When would it be easier to learn a new language, when you were five years old or now? Why?

2. How many times in the last month have you tried something for which the probability of success was less than 50 percent?

3. When was the last time you asked three "why" questions in a row?

~~examples of overcoming the conceptual block of complacency
~thored a book in which he asks and answers more

to their own body odor?

ne guns in a twenty-one-gun salute?

ead that wears off tires?

il or get moldy?

Why doesn't a two- y-four measure two inches by four inches?

Why doesn't postage-stamp glue have flavoring?

Why is the telephone keypad arranged differently from that of a calculator?

Why do hot dogs come ten in a package while buns come eight in a package?

How do military cadets find their caps after throwing them in the air at football games and graduation?

Why is Jack the nickname for John?

How do they print "M&M" on M&M candies?

And so on.

Most of us are a little too complacent to even ask such questions, let alone to find out the answers! We often stop being inquisitive as we get older because we learn that it is good to be intelligent, and being intelligent is interpreted as already knowing the answers (instead of asking good questions). Consequently, we learn less well at thirty-five than at five, take fewer risks, avoid asking why, and function in the world without trying to understand it. Creative problem solvers, on the other hand, are frequently engaged in inquisitive and experimental behavior. Spence Silver at 3M described his attitude about the complacency block this way:

> People like myself get excited about looking for new properties in materials. I find that very satisfying, to perturb the structure slightly and just see what happens. I have a hard time talking people into doing that–people who are more highly trained. It's been my experience that people are reluctant just to try, to experiment–just to see what will happen (Nayak & Ketteringham, 1986, p. 58).

Bias Against Thinking

A second appearance of the complacency block is in an inclination to avoid doing mental work. This block, like most of the others, is partly a cultural bias as well as a personal bias. For example, assume that you passed by your subordinate's office one day and noticed him leaning back in his chair, staring out the window. A half-hour later, as you passed by again, he had his feet up on the desk, still staring out the window. And twenty minutes later, you noticed that his demeanor hadn't changed much. What would be your conclusion? Most of us would assume that the fellow was not doing any work. We would assume that unless we saw action, he wasn't being productive.

When was the last time you heard someone say, "I'm sorry. I can't go to the ball game (or concert, dance, party, or movie) because I have to think?" Or, "I'll do the dishes tonight. I know you need to catch up on your thinking?" That these statements sound humorous illustrates the bias most people develop toward action rather than thought, or against putting their feet up, rocking back in their chair, looking off into space, and engaging in solitary mental activity. This does not mean daydreaming or fantasizing, but *thinking*.

There is a particular conceptual block in our culture against the kind of thinking that uses the right hemisphere of the brain. **Left-hemisphere thinking,** for most people, is concerned with logical, analytic, linear, or sequential tasks. Thinking using the left hemisphere is apt to be organized, planned, and precise. Language and mathematics are left-hemisphere activities. **Right-hemisphere thinking,** on the other hand, is concerned with intuition, synthesis, playfulness, and qualitative judgment. It tends to be more spontaneous, imaginative, and emotional than left-hemisphere thinking. The emphasis in most formal education is toward left-hemisphere thought development. Problem solving on the basis of reason, logic, and utility is generally rewarded, while problem solving based on sentiment, intuition, or pleasure is frequently considered tenuous and inferior.

A number of researchers have found that the most creative problem-solvers are **ambidextrous** in their thinking. That is, they can use both left- and right-hemisphere thinking and easily switch from one to the other (Bruner, 1966; Hermann, 1981; Martindale, 1975). Creative ideas arise most frequently in the right hemisphere but must be processed and interpreted by the left, so creative problem solvers use both hemispheres equally well.

Try the exercise in Table 4, the idea of which came from von Oech (1986). It illustrates this ambidextrous principle. There are two lists of words. Take a minute

Table 4		
Exercise to Test Ambidextrous Thinking		

	LIST 1	LIST 2
	decline	sunset
	very	perfume
	ambiguous	brick
	resources	monkey
	term	castle
	conceptual	guitar
	about	pencil
	appendix	computer
	determine	umbrella
	forget	radar
	quantity	blister
	survey	chessboard

to memorize the first list. Then, on a piece of paper, write down as many words as you can remember. Now take a minute and memorize the words in the second list. Repeat the process of writing down as many words as you can remember.

Most people remember more words from the second list than from the first. This is because the second list contains words that relate to visual perceptions. They connect with right-brain activity as well as left-brain activity. People can draw mental pictures or fantasize about them. The same is true for creative ideas. The more both sides of the brain are used, the more creative the ideas. We will discuss practical ways to do this later.

Review of Conceptual Blocks

So far we have suggested that certain conceptual blocks prevent individuals from solving problems creatively. These blocks, summarized in Table 3, narrow the scope of problem definition, limit the consideration of alternative solutions, and constrain the selection of an optimal solution. Unfortunately, many of these conceptual blocks are unconscious, and it is only by being confronted with problems that are unsolvable because of conceptual blocks that individuals become aware that they exist. We have attempted to make you aware of your own conceptual blocks by asking you to solve problems that require you to overcome these mental barriers. These conceptual blocks, of course, are not all bad; not all problems can be addressed by creative problem solving. But research has shown that individuals who have developed creative problem-solving skills are far more effective with problems that are complex and that require a search for alternative solutions than others who are conceptually blocked (Dauw, 1976; Basadur, 1979; Guilford, 1962; Steiner, 1978).

In the next section we provide some techniques and tools that help overcome these blocks and help improve creative problem-solving skills. In the last section we discuss how creativity and innovation can be fostered in others.

CONCEPTUAL BLOCKBUSTING

Conceptual blocks cannot be overcome all at once because most blocks are a product of years of habit-forming thought processes. Overcoming them requires practice in thinking in different ways over a long period of time. You will not become a skilled creative problem solver, of course, just by reading this module. On the other hand, by becoming aware of your conceptual blocks and practicing the following techniques, you can enhance your creative problem-solving skills.

Stages in Creative Thought

A first step in overcoming conceptual blocks is simply to recognize that creative problem solving is a skill that can be developed. Being a creative problem solver is not a quality that some people have and some don't. As Dauw (1976, p. 19) has noted,

> Research results [show] . . . that nurturing creativity is not a question of increasing one's ability to score high on an IQ test, but a matter of improving

one's mental attitudes and habits and cultivating creative skills that have lain dormant since childhood.

Researchers generally agree that creative problem solving involves four stages: preparation, incubation, illumination, and verification. (See Haefele, 1962, for literature reviews of the stages of creative problem solving.) The **preparation stage** includes gathering data, defining the problem, generating alternatives, and consciously examining all available information. The primary difference between skillful creative problem solving and rational problem solving is in how this first step is approached. Creative problem solvers are more flexible and fluent in data gathering, problem definition, alternative generation, and examination of options. In fact, it is in this stage that training in creative problem solving can significantly improve effectiveness (Allen, 1974; Basadur, 1979; McKim, 1972) because the other three steps are not amenable to conscious mental work. The following discussion, therefore, is limited primarily to improving functioning in this first stage. Second, the **incubation stage** involves mostly unconscious mental activity in which the mind combines unrelated thoughts in the pursuit of a solution. Conscious effort is not involved. **Illumination,** the third stage, occurs when an insight is recognized and a creative solution is articulated. **Verification** is the final stage, which involves evaluating the creative solution relative to some standard of acceptability.

In the preparation stage, two types of techniques are available for improving creative problem-solving abilities. One type helps individuals think about and define the problem more effectively; the other helps individuals gather information and generate more alternative solutions to the problem.

One major difference between effective, creative problem solvers and other people is that creative problem solvers are less constrained. They allow themselves to be more flexible in the definitions they impose on problems and the number of solutions they identify. They develop a large repertoire of approaches to problem solving. In short, they do what Karl Weick (1979, p. 261) prescribes for unblocking decision making: "Complicate yourself!" That is, generate more conceptual options. As Interaction Associates (1971, p. 15) explained:

> Flexibility in thinking is critical to good problem solving. A problem solver should be able to conceptually dance around the problem like a good boxer, jabbing and poking, without getting caught in one place or "fixated." At any given moment, a good problem solver should be able to apply a large number of strategies [for generating alternative definitions and solutions]. Moreover, a good problem solver is a person who has developed, through his understanding of strategies and experiences in problem solving, a sense of appropriateness of what is likely to be the most useful strategy at any particular time.

As a perusal through any bookstore will show, the number of books suggesting ways to enhance creative problem solving is enormous. In the next section we present just a few tools and hints that we have found to be especially effective and relatively simple for executives and students of business to apply. Whereas some of them may seem a little game-like or playful, that is precisely what they are supposed to do—unfreeze you from your normal skeptical, analytical approach to problems and increase your playfulness.

Methods for Improving Problem Definition

Problem definition is probably the most critical step in creative problem solving. Once a problem is defined, solving it is often relatively simple. However, Campbell (1952), Medawar (1967), and Schumacher (1977) point out that individuals tend to define problems in terms with which they are familiar. Medawar (1967, Introduction) notes, "Good scientists study the most important problems they think they can solve." When a problem is faced that is strange or does not appear to have a solution (what Schumacher calls "divergent problems"), the problem either remains undefined or is redefined in terms of something familiar. Unfortunately, new problems may not be the same as old problems, so relying on past definitions may lead to solving the wrong problem. Applying some hints for creative problem definition can help individuals see problems in alternative ways so their definitions are not so narrowly constrained. Three such hints for improving and expanding definition are discussed below.

Make the Strange Familiar and the Familiar Strange

One well-known technique for improving creative problem solving is called **synectics** (Gordon, 1961). The goal of synectics is simply to help you put something you don't know in terms of something you do know and vice versa. By analyzing what you know and applying it to what you don't know, new insights and perspectives can be developed. It works like this.

First you form a definition of a problem (make the strange familiar). Then you try to make that definition out-of-focus, distorted, or transposed in some way (make the familiar strange). Use synectics—analogies and metaphors—to create this distortion. Then you postpone the original definition of the problem while you analyze the analogy or metaphor. You impose the analysis on the original problem to see what new insights you can uncover.

For example, suppose you have defined a problem as low morale among members of your team. You may form an analogy or metaphor by answering questions such as the following about the problem: What does this remind me of? What does this make me feel like? What is this similar to? What *isn't* this similar to? (Your answers, for example, might be: This problem reminds me of trying to turn a rusty bolt. It makes me feel like I do when visiting a hospital ward. This is similar to the loser's locker room after a basketball game. And so on.) Metaphors and analogies should connect what you are less sure about (the original problem) to what you are more sure about (the metaphor). By analyzing the metaphor or analogy, you may identify attributes of the problem that were not evident before. New insights can occur.

Many creative solutions have been generated by such a technique. For example, William Harvey was the first to apply the "pump" analogy to the heart, which led to the discovery of the body's circulation system. Niels Bohr compared the atom to the solar system and supplanted Rutherford's prevailing "raisin pudding" model of matter's building blocks. Creativity consultant Roger von Oech (1986) helped turn around a struggling computer company by applying a restaurant analogy to the company's operations. The real problems became highlighted when the restaurant, rather than the company, was analyzed. Major contributions in the field of organizational behavior have occurred by applying analogies to other types of organization, such as machines, cybernetic or open systems, force fields, clans, and so on. Probably the most effective analogies (called parables) were used by Jesus to teach principles that otherwise were difficult for individuals to grasp, given their culture and heritage.

Some hints to keep in mind when constructing analogies are these: (1) Include action or motion in the analogy (for example, driving a car, cooking a meal, attending a funeral); (2) include things that can be visualized or pictured in the analogy (for example, stars, football games, crowded shopping malls); (3) pick familiar events or situations (for example, families, kissing, bedtime), and (4) try to relate things that are not obviously similar (for example, saying an organization is like a crowd is not nearly so rich a simile as saying an organization is like a psychic prison or a poker game).

Four types of analogies are recommended as part of synectics: **personal analogies,** where individuals try to identify themselves as the problem ("If I were the problem, how would I feel, what would I like, what could satisfy me?"); **direct analogies,** where individuals apply facts, technology, and common experience to the problem (e.g., Brunel solved the problem of underwater construction by watching a shipworm tunneling into a tube); **symbolic analogies,** where symbols or images are imposed on the problem (e.g., modeling the problem mathematically or diagramming the logic flow); and **fantasy analogies,** where individuals ask the question, "In my wildest dreams, how would I wish the problem to be resolved?" (For example, "I wish all employees would work with no supervision.")

Elaborate on the Definition

There are a variety of ways to enlarge, alter, or replace a problem definition once it has been specified. One way is to force yourself to generate at least two alternative hypotheses for every problem definition. That is, specify at least two plausible definitions of the problem in addition to the one originally accepted. Think in plural terms rather than in singular terms. Instead of asking, "What is the problem?" "What is the meaning of this?" "What is the result?" ask instead questions like: "What are the problems?" "What are the meanings of this?" "What are the results?"

As an example, look at Figure 6. Select the figure that is different from all the others. A majority of people select *b* first. If you did, you're right. It is the only figure that has all straight lines. On the other hand, quite a few people pick *a*. If you are one of them, you're also right. It is the only figure with a continuous line—no points of discontinuity. Alternatively, *c* can also be right with the rationale that it is the only figure with two straight and two curved lines. Similarly, *d* is the only one with one curved and one straight line, and *e* is the only figure that is nonsymmetrical or partial. The point is, there can often be more than one problem definition, more than one right answer, and more than one perspective from which to view a problem.

Another way to elaborate definitions is to use a question checklist. This is simply a series of questions designed to help individuals think of alternatives to

Figure 6

The Five-Figure Problem

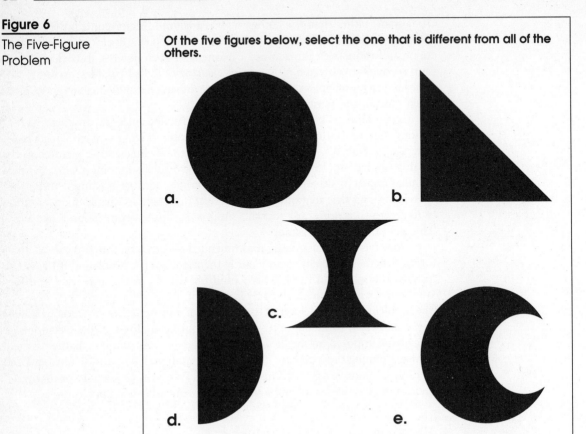

Of the five figures below, select the one that is different from all of the others.

a.

b.

c.

d.

e.

their accepted definitions. Several creative managers have shared with us some of their most fruitful questions:

1. Is there anything else?
2. Is the reverse true?
3. Is there a more general problem?
4. Can it be stated differently?
5. Who sees it differently?
6. What past experience is this like?

As an exercise, take a minute now to think of a problem you are currently experiencing. Write it down so it is formally specified. Now manipulate that definition by answering each of the six questions in the checklist. If you can't think of a problem, try the exercise with this one: "I am not as attractive as I would like to be."

Reverse the Definition

A third tool for improving and expanding problem definition is to reverse the definition of the problem. That is, turn the problem upside down, inside out, or back to front. Reverse the way in which you think of the problem. For example, consider the following problem.

> Many years ago, a small businessman found himself with a large debt to a creditor. The creditor, rumored to have been associated with organized crime, became adamant that repayment be made by a deadline that was impossible for the businessman to meet. Business was not good, and the businessman could not even keep up the interest payments, let alone the loan principal. The creditor, however, had become attracted to the businessman's daughter, and in his conniving ways, decided he would rather have the girl than the small, failing business. The daughter, however, was repulsed by such a suggestion and resisted all his advances.
>
> The creditor was a gambling man and always enjoyed the thrill of a contest. He decided to propose a game to the businessman and his daughter that would decide her fate and that of the business. He indicated that he would put a white pebble and a black pebble into a bag and then have the young woman pick out a pebble. If she chose the black pebble, she would become his wife and the businessman's debt would be considered paid in full. If she chose the white pebble, she could stay with her father and the debt would be cancelled. If she refused to participate in the game, the entire balance would be made due by the end of the month.
>
> Reluctantly, the businessman agreed to the creditor's proposal. They met on a pebble-strewn path in the local arboretum to conduct this game of chance. As they chatted, the creditor stooped down, picked up two pebbles, and put them into a bag. The young woman, sharp-eyed with fright, noticed that the creditor had put two black pebbles in the bag. He held up the bag and asked the young woman to select the pebble that would decide her fate and that of her father's business. (The idea for this puzzle came from deBono, 1968.)

What would you advise the girl to do?

A common approach is to maintain a constant definition of the problem and try to manipulate the circumstances. Most individuals suggest one of these alternatives:

1. The young woman should accuse the creditor of cheating. (But then she risks antagonizing him and having him cancel the game. Her father loses the business.)

2. The young woman should try to change the rules of the contest. (But the creditor is no dummy, and he certainly is not going to make it more difficult for himself to get what he wants.)

3. The young woman should try to cheat by picking up a white pebble from the ground. (But the creditor would certainly not allow her to stoop down and pick up any pebble after he held up the bag and invited her to select one.)

4. She should sacrifice herself and then try to get out of the marriage later.

Each of these suggestions is good, but all of them maintain a single definition of the problem. Each assumes that the solution to the problem is associated with the pebble that the girl selects. If the problem is reversed, other answers normally not considered become evident. That is, the pebble remaining in the bag could also determine her fate.

In the story, the girl selects a pebble from the bag, but then quickly drops it to the ground on the pebble-strewn path. She exclaims, "Oh, how clumsy of me. But never mind, if you will look into the bag at the remaining pebble, the color of the pebble I chose will be obvious." By reversing the definition, she changed a situation with zero probability of success to a situation with 100 percent probability of success.

This reversal is similar to what Rothenberg (1979) refers to as "Janusian thinking." Janus was the Roman god with two faces that looked in opposite directions. **Janusian thinking** means thinking contradictory thoughts at the same time—that is, conceiving two opposing ideas to be true concurrently. Rothenberg claimed, after studying fifty-four highly creative artists and scientists (e.g., Nobel Prize winners), that most major scientific breakthroughs and artistic masterpieces are products of Janusian thinking. Creative people who actively formulate antithetical ideas and then resolve them produce the most valuable contributions to the scientific and artistic worlds. Quantum leaps in knowledge often occur.

An example is Einstein's account (1919, p. 1) of having "the happiest thought of my life." He developed the concept that, "for an observer in free fall from the roof of a house, there exists, during his fall, no gravitational field . . . in his immediate vicinity. If the observer releases any objects, they will remain, relative to him, in a state of rest. The [falling] observer is therefore justified in considering his state as one of rest." Einstein concluded, in other words, that two seemingly contradictory states could be present simultaneously: motion and rest. This realization led to the development of his revolutionary general theory of relativity.

In another study of creative potential, Rothenberg (1979) found that when individuals were presented with a stimulus word and asked to respond with the word that first came to mind, highly creative students, Nobel scientists, and prize-winning artists responded with antonyms significantly more often than did individuals with average creativity. Rothenberg argued, based on these results, that creative people think in terms of opposites more often than do other people.

For our purposes, the whole point is to reverse or contradict the currently accepted definition in order to expand the number of perspectives considered. For instance, a problem might be that morale is too high instead of (or in addition to) too low in our team, or that employees need less motivation instead of more motivation to increase productivity. Opposites and backward looks often enhance creativity.

These three techniques for improving creative problem definition are summarized in Table 5. Their purpose is not to help you generate alternative definitions just for the sake of alternatives but to broaden your perspectives, to help

Table 5

Techniques for
Improving Problem
Definition

1. Make the strange familiar and the familiar strange.
2. Elaborate on the definition.
3. Reverse the definition.

you overcome conceptual blocks, and to produce more elegant (high-quality and parsimonious) solutions.

Generate More Alternatives

A common tendency is to define problems in terms of available solutions (i.e., the problem is defined as a solution already possessed or the first acceptable alternative (e.g., March & Simon, 1958). This tendency leads to consideration of a minimal number and narrow range of alternatives in problem solving. However, Guilford (1962), a pioneer in the study of creative problem solving, asserted that the primary characteristics of effective creative problem solvers are their fluency and their flexibility of thought. **Fluency** refers to the number of ideas or concepts produced in a given length of time. **Flexibility** refers to the diversity of ideas or concepts generated. While most problem solvers consider a few homogeneous alternatives, creative problem solvers consider many heterogeneous alternatives. The following techniques are designed to help you improve your ability to generate many varied alternatives when faced with problems. They are summarized in Table 6.

Defer Judgment

Probably the most common method of generating alternatives is the technique of **brainstorming** developed by Osborn (1953). This tool is powerful because most people make quick judgments about each piece of information or each alternative solution they encounter. This technique is designed to help people generate alternatives for problem solving without prematurely evaluating, and hence discarding, them. Four main rules govern brainstorming:

1. No evaluation of any kind is permitted as alternatives are being generated. Individual energy is spent on generating ideas, not on defending them.

2. The wildest possible ideas are encouraged. It is easier to tighten alternatives up than to loosen them.

3. The quantity of ideas takes precedence over the quality. Emphasizing quality engenders judgment and evaluation.

4. Participants should build on or modify the ideas of others. Poor ideas that are added to or altered often become good ideas.

Brainstorming techniques are best used in a group setting so individuals can stimulate ideas in one another. In fact, generating alternatives in a group setting produces more and better ideas than can be produced alone (Maier, 1967). One

Table 6 Techniques for Generating More Alternatives	1. Defer judgment. 2. Expand current alternatives. 3. Combine unrelated attributes.

caution about brainstorming should be noted, however. Often, after a rush of alternatives is produced at the outset of a brainstorming session, the quantity of ideas rapidly subsides. But to stop there is an ineffective use of brainstorming. When no easily identifiable solutions are available, truly creative alternatives are often produced in brainstorming groups. So keep working!

The best way to get a feel for the power of brainstorming groups is to participate in one. Try the following exercise based on an actual problem faced by a group of students and university professors. Spend at least twenty minutes in a small group, brainstorming ideas.

> An executive education program for mid-level managers at a major automobile company had been requested that would focus on enhancing their creativity and innovation. The trouble was, the top human resource executive indicated that he did not want to approach the subject with "brain-teaser" examples. Instead he wanted some other approaches used that would help these managers become more creative personally and more effective at fostering innovation among others.

What ideas can you come up with for how to teach this subject to mid-level managers in an organization? How could you help them learn to be more creative? Generate as many ideas as you can following the rules of brainstorming. After at least twenty minutes, assess the fluency and flexibility of the ideas generated.

Expand Current Alternatives

Sometimes brainstorming in a group is not possible or is too costly in terms of the number of people involved and hours required. Managers pursuing a hectic organizational life may sometimes find brainstorming an unusable alternative. Moreover, people sometimes need an external stimulus or blockbuster to help them generate new ideas. One useful technique for expanding the alternatives that is readily available is the technique of **subdivision.** Subdivision means simply dividing a problem into smaller parts. March and Simon (1958, p. 193) suggest that subdivision improves problem solving by increasing the speed with which alternatives can be generated and selected. As they explain,

> The mode of subdivision has an influence on the extent to which planning can proceed simultaneously on the several aspects of the problem. The more detailed the factorization of the problem, the more simultaneous activity is possible, hence, the greater the speed of problem solving.

To see how subdivision helps develop more alternatives and speeds the process of problem solving, consider the problem, common in the creativity literature, of listing alternative uses for a familiar object. For example, in five minutes, how many uses can you list for a ping-pong ball? The more uses you list, the greater is your *fluency* in thinking. The more variety in the list, the greater is your *flexibility* in thinking. You might include the following in your list: bob for a fishing line, Christmas ornament, toy for a cat, gearshift knob, model for a molecular structure, wind gauge when hung from a string, head for a finger puppet, miniature basketball. Your list will be much longer.

After you generate your list, apply the technique of subdivision by identifying the specific characteristics of a ping-pong ball—that is, dividing it into its component attributes. For example, weight, color, texture, shape, porosity, strength, hardness, chemical properties, and conduction potential are all attributes of ping-pong balls that help expand the uses you might think of. By dividing an object mentally into more specific attributes, you can arrive at many more alternative uses (e.g., reflector, holder when cut in half, bug bed, ball for lottery drawing, and so on).

One exercise we have sometimes used with students and executives to illustrate this technique is to have them write down as many of their managerial strengths as they can think of. Most people list ten or twelve attributes relatively easily. Then we analyze the various dimensions of the manager's role, the activities that managers engage in, the challenges that most managers face from inside and outside the organization, and so on. We then ask these same people to write down another list of their strengths as managers. The list is almost always twice as long or more. The point is, by identifying the subcomponents of any problem, far more alternatives can be generated than by considering the problem as a whole.

One final illustration. Divide the figure in Figure 7 into exactly four pieces equal in size, shape, and area. Try to do it in a minute or less. The problem is easy if you use subdivision. It is more difficult if you don't. One of the answers to the problem is in Appendix I, page 91.

Combine Unrelated Attributes

A third technique focuses on helping problem solvers expand alternatives by forcing the integration of seemingly unrelated elements. Research into creative problem

Figure 7

Fractionation
Problem

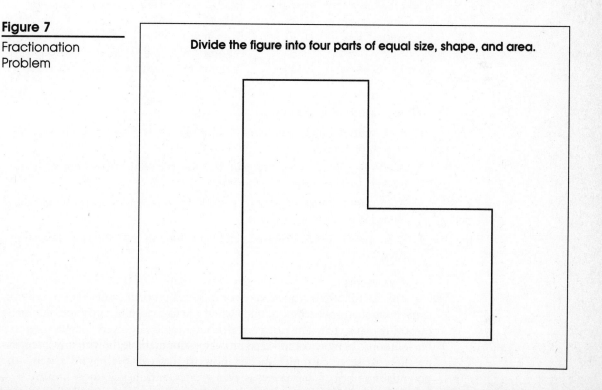

Divide the figure into four parts of equal size, shape, and area.

solving has shown that an ability to see common relationships among disparate factors is a major factor differentiating creative individuals from noncreative (see Dellas & Gaier, 1970, for a review of the literature). Two ways to do this are through **morphological forced connections** (Koberg & Bagnall, 1974) and the **relational algorithm** (Crovitz, 1970).

With morphological forced connections, a four-step procedure is involved. First, the problem is written down. Second, attributes of the problem are listed. Third, alternatives to each attribute are listed. Fourth, different alternatives from the attributes list are combined together.

To illustrate this procedure, suppose you are faced with the problem of a secretary who takes an extended lunch break almost every day despite your reminders to be on time. Think of alternative ways to solve this problem. The first solution that comes to mind for most people is to sit down and have a talk with (or threaten) the secretary. If that doesn't work, most of us would just fire or transfer the person. However, look at what other alternatives can be generated by using morphological connections:

STEP 1:   **Problem statement:** The secretary takes extended lunch breaks every day with friends in the cafeteria.

STEP 2:   **Major attributes of the problem:**

Amount of time	Start time	Place	With whom	Frequency
More than 1 hour	12 noon	Cafeteria	Friends	Daily

STEP 3:   **Alternative attributes:**

Amount of time	Start time	Place	With whom	Frequency
30 minutes	11:00	Office	Co-workers	Weekly
90 minutes	11:30	Conference Room	Boss	Twice a Week
45 minutes	12:30	Restaurant	Management Team	Alternate Days

STEP 4:   **Combining Attributes:**

1. A 30-minute lunch beginning at 12:30 in the conference room with the boss once a week.

2. A 90-minute lunch beginning at 11:30 in the conference room with co-workers twice a week.

3. A 45-minute lunch beginning at 11:00 in the cafeteria with the management team every other day.

4. A 30-minute lunch beginning at 12:00 alone in the office on alternate days.

And so forth.

This is, admittedly, not a very complicated problem, but you can see how many more alternatives come to mind when you force together attributes that aren't obviously connected. The matrix of attributes can create a very long list of possible solutions. In more complicated problems—for example, how to improve quality, how to serve customers better, how to improve the reward system—the potential number of alternatives is even greater, and, hence, more creative.

A second technique for combining unrelated attributes in problem solving is the *relational algorithm*. This involves applying connecting words that force a relationship between two elements in a problem. For example, the following is a list of some relational words:

about	among	because	by	if	now
across	and	before	down	in	of
after	as	between	for	near	off
against	at	but	from	not	on
opposite	over	so	through	under	where
or	round	then	till	up	while
out	still	though	to	when	with

To illustrate the use of this technique, suppose you are faced with the following problem: Our customers are dissatisfied with our service. The two major elements in this problem are *customers* and *service*. They are connected by the phrase *are dissatisfied with*. With the relational algorithm technique, the relational words in the problem statement are removed and replaced with other relational words to see if new ideas for alternative solutions can be identified. For example, consider the following connections where new relational words are used:

- Customers *among* service (e.g., Customers interact with service personnel.)
- Customers *as* service (e.g., Customers deliver service to other customers.)
- Customers *and* service (e.g., Customers and service personnel work together.)
- Customers *for* service (e.g., Customer focus groups help improve our service.)
- Service *near* customers (e.g., Change the location of the service.)
- Service *before* customers (e.g., Prepare service before the customer arrives.)
- Service *through* customers (e.g., Use customers to provide additional service.)
- Service *when* customers (e.g., Provide timely service.)

By connecting the two elements of the problem in different ways, new possibilities for problem solution can be formulated.

Hints for Applying Problem-Solving Techniques

Not every problem is amenable to these techniques and tools for conceptual blockbusting, of course. But our intent in presenting these six is to help you expand the number of options available to you for defining problems and for generating additional potential solutions. They are most useful when problems arise that require a new approach or a new perspective. All of us have enormous creative potential, but the stresses and pressures of daily life, coupled with the inertia of conceptual habits, tend to submerge that potential. These hints are merely ways to help unlock it again.

Reading about techniques or wanting to be creative won't improve your creativity, of course. These techniques and tools are not magic in themselves. They depend on your ability to actually generate new ideas and to think different thoughts. Because that is so difficult for most of us, here are six practical hints to help prepare you to create more conceptual flexibility and to better apply these techniques.

1. Give yourself some relaxation time.
   The more intense your work, the more your need for complete breaks. Break out of your routine sometimes. This frees up your mind and gives room for new thoughts.

2. Find a place (physical space) where you can think.
   It should be a place where interruptions are eliminated, at least for a time. Reserve your best time for thinking.

3. Talk to other people about ideas.
   Isolation produces far fewer ideas than does conversation. Make a list of people who stimulate you to think. Spend some time with them.

4. Ask other people for their ideas about your problems.
   Find out what others think about them. Don't be embarrassed to share your problems, but don't become dependent on others to solve them for you.

5. Read a lot.
   Read at least one thing regularly that is outside your field of expertise. Keep track of new thoughts from your reading.

6. Protect yourself from idea-killers.
   Don't spend time with "black holes"—people who absorb all of your energy and light but give nothing in return. Don't let yourself or others negatively evaluate your ideas too soon.

You'll find these hints useful not only for enhancing creative problem solving but for rational problem solving as well. Figure 8 summarizes the two problem-solving processes—rational and creative—and the factors you should consider when determining how to approach each type of problem. In brief, when you encounter a problem that is straightforward—that is, outcomes are predictable, sufficient information is available, and means-ends connections are clear—rational problem-solving techniques are most appropriate. You should apply the four distinct, sequential steps. On the other hand, when the problem is not straightforward—that is, information is ambiguous and/or unavailable and alternative solutions are not apparent—you should apply creative problem-solving techniques in order to improve problem definition and alternative generation.

FOSTERING INNOVATION

Unlocking your own creative potential is not enough, of course, to make you a successful manager. A major challenge is to help unlock it in other people as well. Fostering innovation and creativity among those with whom you work is at least as great a challenge as increasing your own creativity. In this last section of the

Figure 8 A Model of Rational and Creative Problem Solving

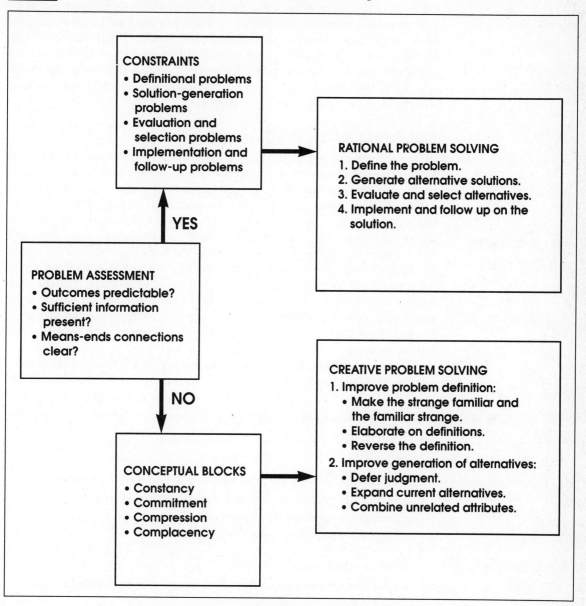

module, we briefly discuss some principles that will help you better accomplish the task of fostering innovation.

Management Principles for Innovativeness

Neither Percy Spencer nor Spence Silver could have succeeded in their creative ideas had there not been a managerial support system present that fostered creative problem solving and the pursuit of innovation. In each case, certain characteristics were present in their organizations—fostered by managers around them—that made their innovations possible. In this section we will not discuss the macro-organizational issues associated with innovation—e.g., organization design, strategic orientation, and human resource systems. Excellent discussions of those factors are reviewed in sources such as Galbraith (1982), Kanter (1983), McMillan (1985), Tichy (1983), and Amabile (1988). Instead, we'll focus on some of the activities in which individual managers can engage that foster innovativeness. Table 7 summarizes three management principles that can help engender more innovativeness and creative problem solving.

Pull People Apart; Put People Together

Percy Spencer's magnetron project was a consumer product closeted away from Raytheon's main-line business of missiles and other defense contract work. Spence Silver's new glue resulted when a polymer adhesive task force was separated from 3M's normal activities. The Macintosh computer was developed by a task force that was taken outside the company and given space and time to work on an innovative computer. Many new ideas come from individuals being given some time and resources and allowed to work apart from the normal activities of the organization. Establishing bullpens, practice fields, or sandlots is as good a way to develop new skills in business as it has proven to be in athletics. Because most businesses are designed to produce the 10,000th part correctly or to service the 10,000th customer efficiently, they do not function very well at producing the first part. That is why pulling people apart is often necessary to foster innovation and creativity.

On the other hand, forming teams (putting people together) is almost always more productive than people working by themselves. But the teams should be

Table 7 Three Principles for Fostering Innovativeness

PRINCIPLE	EXAMPLES
1. Pull people apart; Put people together.	■ Let individuals work alone as well as with teams and task forces. ■ Encourage minority reports and legitimize "devil's advocate" roles. ■ Encourage heterogeneous membership in teams. ■ Separate competing groups or subgroups.
2. Monitor and prod.	■ Talk to customers. ■ Identify customer expectations both in advance and after the sale. ■ Hold people accountable. ■ Use "sharp-pointed" prods.
3. Reward multiple roles.	■ Idea champion ■ Sponsor and mentor ■ Orchestrator and facilitator ■ Rule breaker

characterized by certain attributes. For example, Nemeth (1986) found that creativity increased markedly when minority influences were present in the team, for example, when "devil's advocate" roles were legitimized, a formal minority report was always included in final recommendations, and individuals assigned to work on a team had divergent backgrounds or views. "Those exposed to minority views are stimulated to attend to more aspects of the situation, they think in more divergent ways, and they are more likely to detect novel solutions or to come to new decisions" (Nemeth, 1986, p. 25). Nemeth found that those positive benefits occur in groups even when the divergent or minority views are wrong. Similarly, Janis (1971) found that narrow-mindedness in groups (called groupthink) was best overcome by establishing competing groups working on the same problem, participation in groups by outsiders, assigning a role of critical evaluator in the group, having groups made up of cross-functional participants, and so on. The most productive groups are those that are characterized by fluid roles, lots of interaction among members, and flat power structures.

The point is, innovativeness can be fostered when individuals are placed in teams and when they are at least temporarily separated from the normal pressures of organizational life. Those teams, however, are most effective at generating innovative ideas when they are characterized by attributes of minority influence, competition, heterogeneity, and interaction. You can help foster innovation among people you manage, therefore, by pulling people apart (e.g., give them a bullpen) as well as putting people together (e.g., put them on a team).

Monitor and Prod

Neither Percy Spencer nor Spence Silver were allowed to work on their projects with no accountability. Both men eventually had to report on the results they accomplished with their experimentation and imagination. At 3M, for example, people are *expected* to steal 15 percent of their time away from company business to work on new, creative ideas. They can even appropriate company materials and resources to work on them. However, individuals are always held accountable for their lawlessness. They need to show results for their "play time."

Holding people accountable for outcomes, in fact, is an important motivator for improved performance. Two innovators in the entertainment industry captured this principle with these remarks: "The ultimate inspiration is the deadline. That's when you have to do what needs to be done. The fact that twice a year the creative talent of this country is working until midnight to get something ready for a trade show is very good for the economy. Without this kind of pressure, things would turn to mashed potatoes" (von Oech, 1986, p. 119).

In addition to accountability, innovativeness is stimulated by what Gene Goodson at Johnson Controls called "sharp-pointed prods." After taking over the automotive group at that company, Goodson found that he could stimulate creative problem solving by issuing certain mandates that demanded innovativeness. One such mandate was, "There will be no more forklift trucks allowed in any of our plants." At first hearing, that mandate sounds absolutely outrageous. Think about it. You have a plant with tens of thousands of square feet of floor space. The loading docks are on one side of the building, and many tons of heavy metal raw materials are unloaded weekly and moved from the loading docks to work stations throughout the entire facility. The only way it can be done is with forklifts. Eliminating forklift trucks would ruin the plant, right? Wrong. This sharp-pointed prod simply demanded that individuals working in the plant find ways to move the work stations closer to the raw materials, to move the unloading of the raw materials closer to the work stations, or to change the size and amounts of material being unloaded. The innovations that resulted from eliminating forklifts saved the company millions of dollars in materials handling and wasted time, dramatically improved quality, productivity, and efficiency, and made it possible for Johnson Controls to capture some business from their Japanese competitors.

One of the best methods for generating useful prods is to regularly monitor customer preferences, expectations, and evaluations. Many of the most creative ideas have come from customers, the recipients of goods and services. Identifying their preferences in advance and monitoring their evaluations of products or services later are both good ways to get ideas for innovation and to be prodded to make improvements. All employees should be in regular contact with their own customers, asking questions and monitoring performance.

By customers, we don't mean just the end-users of a business product or service. In fact, all of us have customers, whether we are students in school, members of a family, players on a basketball team, or whatever. Customers are simply those for whom we are trying to produce something or whom we serve. Students, for example, can count their instructors, fellow class members, and potential employers as customers whom they serve. A priori and post hoc monitoring of their expectations and evaluations is an important way to help foster new ideas for problem solving. This monitoring is best done through one-on-one meetings (see the module *Communicating Supportively*, which discusses the Personal Management Interview Program), but it can also be done through followup calls, surveys, customer complaint cards, suggestion systems, and so on.

The basic point is simply that you can foster innovativeness by holding people accountable for new ideas and by stimulating them with periodic prods. The most useful prods generally come from customers.

Reward Multiple Roles

The success of the sticky yellow notes at 3M is more than a story of the creativity of Spence Silver. In fact, without a number of people playing multiple roles, the glue would probably still be on a shelf somewhere. Instead, it provides a good illustration of the necessity of multiple roles in innovation and the importance of recognizing and rewarding them. Four crucial roles in the innovative process are the **idea champion** (the person who comes up with the innovative problem solution), the **sponsor** or **mentor** (the person who helps provide the resources, environment, and encouragement for the idea champion to work on the idea), the **orchestrator** or **facilitator** (the person who brings together cross-functional groups and necessary political support to facilitate implementation of the creative idea), and the **rule breaker** (the person who goes beyond organizational boundaries and barriers to ensure success of the innovation). Each of these roles is present in most important innovations in organizations, and they are illustrated by the Post-It Note example below.

This story has four major parts.

1. Spence Silver, by fooling around with chemical configurations that the academic literature indicated wouldn't work, invented a glue that wouldn't stick. He stuck with it, however, and spent years giving presentations to any audience at 3M that would listen, trying to pawn it off on some division that could find a practical application for it. The trouble was, no one else got stuck on it.

2. Henry Courtney and Roger Merrill developed a coating substance that allowed the glue to stick to one surface but not to others. This made it possible to produce a permanently temporary glue–that is, one that would peel off easily when pulled but would otherwise hang on forever.

3. Art Fry found the problem that fit Spence Silver's solution. He found application for the glue as a "better bookmark" and as a note pad. The trouble was, no equipment existed at 3M to coat only a part of a piece of paper with the glue. Fry, therefore, carried 3M equipment and tools home to his own basement, where he designed and made his own machine to manufacture the forerunner of Post-It Notes. Because the working machine became too large to get out of his basement, he blasted a hole in the wall to get the equipment back to 3M. He then brought together engineers, designers, production managers, and machinists to demonstrate the prototype machine and generate enthusiasm for beginning to manufacture the product.

4. Geoffrey Nicholson and Joseph Ramsey began marketing the product inside 3M. They also submitted the product to the standard 3M market tests. The trouble was, the product failed miserably. No one wanted to pay $1.00 for a pad of scratch paper. However, they broke 3M rules by personally visiting test market sites and giving away free samples. Only then did the consuming public become addicted to the product.

This brief scenario illustrates the importance of these four roles in the innovation process. Spence Silver was both a rule breaker and an idea champion. Art Fry was also an idea champion, but more importantly, he orchestrated the coming together of the various groups needed to get the innovation off the ground. Henry Courtney and Roger Merrill helped sponsor Silver's innovation by providing him with the coating substance that would allow his idea to work. And Geoff Nicholson and Joe Ramsey were both rule breakers and sponsors in their bid to get the product accepted by the public. In each case, not only did all these people play unique roles, but they did so with tremendous enthusiasm and zeal. They were both confident of their ideas and willing to put their time and resources on the line as advocates. They fostered support among a variety of constituencies both within their own areas of expertise as well as among outside groups. Most organizations are inclined to give in to those who are sure of themselves, persistent in their efforts, and savvy enough to make converts of others.

Not everyone can be an idea champion. But when managers also reward and recognize those who sponsor and orchestrate the ideas of others, innovativeness increases in organizations. Teams form, supporters replace competitors, and creativity thrives. Facilitating multiple role development is the job of the innovative manager.

SUMMARY

In the last fifteen years, the growth rate of new patent applications in this country has declined by 25 percent. Last year almost half of the patents issued in America were given to foreigners. One major U.S. corporation reported that five years ago over 70 percent of its licensing agreements consisted of patents it sold to other countries. Now it purchases over half its products using licensing agreements from foreign countries. America marketed 82 percent of the world's inventions twenty-five years ago, but it now ranks behind several other countries in new-product introductions. Even without the well-developed medical and pharmaceutical school system existing in the U.S., for example, Japan has still led the world in the introductions of new drugs for the last five years. One U.S. automobile manufacturer bragged of receiving over 30,000 suggestions for improvement from employees in one year; then a Japanese rival opened a plant fifty miles away and received over 3 million suggestions from employees in a single year. In short, the U.S. has experienced a decline in creativity and innovation in the last several years. Flexibility in thinking and effective management problem solving seem to have taken a nose-dive.

As we have pointed out, a well-developed model exists for solving problems. It consists of four separate and sequential stages: defining the problem; generating alternative solutions; evaluating and selecting a solution; and implementing it and following it up. This model, however, is mainly useful for solving straightforward problems. Many problems faced by managers are not of this type, and frequently managers are called on to exercise creative problem-solving skills. That is, they must broaden their perspective of the problem and develop alternative solutions that are not immediately obvious.

We have discussed and illustrated eight major conceptual blocks that inhibit most people's creative problem-solving abilities. Conceptual blocks are mental obstacles that artificially constrain problem definition and solution and that keep most people from being effective creative problem solvers. The four major conceptual blocks are summarized in Table 3.

Overcoming these conceptual blocks is a matter of skill development and practice in thinking, not a matter of innate ability. Everyone can become a skilled creative problem solver with practice. Becoming aware of these thinking inhibiters helps individuals overcome them. We also discussed three major principles for improving creative problem definition and three major principles for improving the creative generation of alternative solutions. Certain techniques were described that can help implement these six principles.

We concluded by offering some hints about how to foster creativity and innovativeness among other people. Becoming an effective problem solver yourself is important, but effective managers can also enhance this activity among their subordinates, peers, and superiors.

BEHAVIORAL GUIDELINES

Below are specific behavioral action guidelines to help your skill practice in problem solving, creativity, and fostering innovation.

1. Follow the four-step procedure outlined in Table 1 when solving straight-forward problems. Keep the steps separate, and do not take short cuts.

2. When approaching a difficult problem, try to overcome your conceptual blocks by consciously doing the following mental activities:

   - Use lateral thinking in addition to vertical thinking.
   - Use several thought languages instead of just one.
   - Challenge stereotypes based on past experiences.
   - Identify underlying themes and commonalities in seemingly unrelated factors.
   - Delete superfluous information and fill in important missing information when studying the problem.
   - Avoid artificially constraining problem boundaries.
   - Ignore reticence to be inquisitive.
   - Use both right- and left-brain thinking.

3. When defining a problem, make the strange familiar and the familiar strange by using metaphor and analogy first to focus and then to distort and refocus the definition.

4. Elaborate the problem definitions by developing at least two alternative (opposite) definitions and by applying a checklist.

5. Reverse the problem definition by beginning with the end result and working backwards.

6. In generating potential problem solutions, defer judging any until many have been proposed. Use the four rules of brainstorming:

   - Do not evaluate.
   - Encourage wild ideas.
   - Encourage quantity.
   - Build on others' ideas.

7. Expand the list of current alternative solutions by subdividing the problem into its attributes.

8. Increase the number of possible solutions by combining unrelated problem attributes. Morphological connections and relational algorithms may be helpful.

9. Foster innovativeness among those with whom you work by doing the following:

   ■ Find a "practice field" where individuals can experiment and try out ideas, and assign them responsibility for fostering innovation.

   ■ Put people holding different perspectives in teams to work on problems.

   ■ Hold people accountable for innovation.

   ■ Use sharp-pointed prods to stimulate new thinking.

   ■ Recognize, reward, and encourage the participation of multiple players, including idea champion, sponsor, orchestrator, and rule breaker.

SKILL ANALYSIS

CASES INVOLVING PROBLEM SOLVING

Admiral Kimmel's Failure at Pearl Harbor

In the summer of 1941, as relations between the United States and Japan were rapidly deteriorating, Admiral Kimmel, Commander in Chief of the Pacific Fleet, received many warnings concerning the imminence of war. During this period he worked out a plan in collaboration with his staff at Pearl Harbor, which gave priority to training key personnel and supplying basic equipment to U.S. outposts in the Far East. The plan took account of the possibility of a long, hard war with Japan and the difficulties of mobilizing scarce resources in manpower and material. At that time, Admiral Kimmel and his staff were keenly aware of the risks of being unprepared for war with Japan, as well as of the high costs and risks involved in preparing for war. They appear to have been relatively optimistic about being able to develop a satisfactory military plan and about having sufficient time in which to implement it. In short, all the conditions were present for vigilance, and it seems likely that this coping pattern characterized their planning activity.

But during the late fall of 1941, as the warnings became increasingly more ominous, a different pattern of coping behavior emerged. Admiral Kimmel and his staff continued to cling to the policy to which they had committed themselves, discounting each fresh warning and failing to note that more and more signs were pointing to Pearl Harbor as a possible target for a surprise air attack. They repeatedly renewed their decision to continue using the available resources primarily for training green sailors and soldiers and for supplying bases close to Japan, rather than instituting an adequate alert that would give priority to defending Pearl Harbor against enemy attack.

Knowing that their sector and the rest of the U.S. military organization were not ready for a shooting war, they clung to an unwarranted set of rationalizations. The Japanese, they thought, would not launch an attack against any American possession; and if by some remote chance they decided to do so, it certainly wouldn't be at Pearl Harbor. Admiral Kimmel and his staff acknowledged that Japan could launch a surprise attack in any direction, but remained convinced that it would not be launched in their direction. They saw no reason to change their course. Therefore, they continued to give peacetime weekend leave to the majority of the naval forces in Hawaii and allowed the many warships in the Pacific Fleet to remain anchored at Pearl Harbor, as sitting ducks. Kimmel regularly discussed each warning with members of his staff. At times he became emotionally aroused and obtained reassurance from the members of his in-group. He shared with them a number of rationalizations that bolstered his decision to ignore the warnings. On November 27, 1941, for example, he received an explicit "war warning" from the chief of naval operations in Washington, which stirred up his concern but did not impel him to take any new protective action. This message was intended as a strong follow-up to an earlier warning, which Kimmel had received only three days earlier, stating that war with Japan was imminent and that "a surprise aggressive movement in any direction, including attack on Philippines or Guam, is a possibility." The new warning asserted that "an aggressive move by Japan is expected within the next few days" and instructed Kimmel to "execute appropriate defensive deployment" preparatory to carrying out the naval war plan. The threat conveyed by this warning was evidently strong enough to induce Kimmel to engage in prolonged discussion with his staff about what should be done. But their vigilance seems to have been confined to paying careful attention to the way the warning was worded. During the meeting, members of the staff pointed out to Kimmel that Hawaii was not specifically mentioned as a possible target in either of the two war warnings, whereas other places—the Philippines, Malaya, and other remote areas—were explicitly named. Kimmel went along with the interpretation that the ambiguities they had detected in the wording must have meant that Pearl Harbor was not supposed to be regarded as a likely target, even though the message seemed to be saying that it was. The defensive quality that entered into this judgment is revealed by the fact that Kimmel made no effort to use his available channels of communication in Washington to find out what really had been meant. He ended up agreeing with the members of his advisory group that "there was no chance of a surprise air attack on Hawaii at that particular time."

Since he judged Pearl Harbor not to be vulnerable, Kimmel decided that the limited-alert condition that had been instituted months earlier would be sufficient. He assumed, however, that all U.S. Army units in Hawaii had gone on a full alert in response to this war warning, so that antiaircraft and radar units under army control would be fully activated. But, again, reflecting his defensive lack of interest in carrying out tasks that required acknowledging the threat, Kimmel failed to inquire of Army headquarters exactly what was being done. As a result, he did not discover until after the disaster on December 7 that the Army, too, was on only a limited alert, designed exclusively to protect military installations against local sabotage.

On December 3, 1941, Kimmel engaged in intensive discussion with two members of his staff upon receiving a fresh warning from naval headquarters in Washington stating that U.S. cryptographers had decoded a secret message from Tokyo to all diplomatic missions in the United States and other countries, ordering them to destroy their secret codes. Kimmel realized that this type of order could mean that Japan was making last-minute preparations before launching an attack against the United States. Again, he and his advisers devoted considerable attention to the exact wording of this new, worrisome warning. They made much of the fact that the dispatch said "most" of the codes but not "all." They concluded that the destruction of the codes should be interpreted as a routine precautionary measure and not as a sign that Japan was planning to attack an American possession. Again, no effort was made to find out from Washington how the intelligence units there interpreted the message. But the lengthy discussions and the close attention paid to the wording of these messages imply that they did succeed in at least temporarily inducing decisional conflict.

By December 6, 1941, the day before the attack, Kimmel was aware of a large accumulation of extremely ominous signs. In addition to receiving the official war warnings during the preceding week, he had received a private letter three days earlier from Admiral Stark in Washington stating that both President Roosevelt and Secretary of State Hull now thought that the Japanese were getting ready to launch a surprise attack. Then on December 6, Kimmel received another message from Admiral Stark containing emergency war orders pertaining to the destruction of secret and confidential documents in American bases on outlying Pacific islands. On that same day, the FBI in Hawaii informed Kimmel that the local Japanese consulate had been burning its papers for the last two days. Furthermore, Kimmel's chief naval intelligence officer had reported to him that day, as he had on the preceding days, that despite fresh efforts to pick up Japanese naval signal calls, the whereabouts of all six of Japan's aircraft carriers still remained a mystery. (U.S. Naval Combat Intelligence had lost track of the Japanese aircraft carriers in mid-November, when they started to move toward Hawaii for the planned attack on Pearl Harbor.)

Although the various warning signs, taken together, clearly indicated that Japan was getting ready to launch an attack against the United States, they remained ambiguous as to exactly where the attack was likely to be. There was also considerable "noise" mixed in with the warning signals, including intelligence reports that huge Japanese naval forces were moving toward Malaya. But, inexplicably, there was a poverty of imagination on the part of Kimmel and his staff with regard to considering the possibility that Pearl Harbor itself might be one of the targets of a Japanese attack.

The accumulated warnings, however, were sufficiently impressive to Kimmel to generate considerable concern. On the afternoon of December 6, as he was pondering alternative courses of action, he openly expressed his anxiety to two of his staff officers. He told them he was worried about the safety of the fleet at Pearl Harbor in view of all the disturbing indications that Japan was getting ready for a massive attack somewhere. One member of the staff immediately reassured him that "the Japanese could not possibly be able to proceed in force against Pearl Harbor when they had so much strength concentrated in their Asiatic operations." Another told him that the limited-alert condition he had ordered many weeks earlier would certainly be sufficient and nothing more was needed. "We finally decided," Kimmel subsequently recalled, "that what we had [already] done was still good and we would stick to it." At the end of the discussion Kimmel "put his worries aside" and went off to a dinner party.

SOURCE: Janis & Mann, 1977, p. 120–123.

Discussion Questions

1. What conceptual blocks are illustrated in this case?
2. Outline the problem-solving steps followed by Kimmel and his advisors. What steps in rational problem solving were skipped or short-circuited?
3. What kinds of conceptual blockbusters could have been useful to Kimmel? If you were his advisor, what would you have suggested to help his problem-solving processes?
4. If you knew then what you know now, how would you have redesigned Kimmel's structures and processes so that effective problem solving could occur?

The Sony Walkman

They had been disappointed at first, but it wasn't something that was going to keep them awake nights. Mitsuro Ida and a group of electronics engineers in Sony Corporation's Tape Recorder Division in Tokyo had tried to redesign a small, portable tape recorder, called "Pressman," so that it gave out stereophonic sounds. A year or so before, Ida and his group had been responsible for inventing the first Pressman, a wonderfully compact machine—ideal for use by journalists—which had sold very well.

But the sound in that tape machine was monaural. The next challenge for Sony's tape recorder engineers was to make a portable machine just as small, but with stereophonic sound. The very first stereo Pressman they made, in the last few months of 1978, didn't succeed. When Ida and his colleagues got the stereo circuits into the Pressman chassis (5.25 inches by 3.46 inches, and only 1.14 inches deep), they didn't have any space left to fit in the recording mechanism. They had made a stereophonic tape recorder that couldn't record anything. Ida regarded this as a good first try but a useless product. But he didn't throw it away. The stereo Pressman was a nice little machine. So the engineers found a few favorite music cassettes and played them while they worked.

After Ida and his fellow designers had turned their nonrecording tape recorder into background music, they didn't entirely ignore it. They had frequent discussions about how to fit the stereo function and the recording mechanism into that overly small space. It was not an easy problem to solve, but because of that it was all the more fascinating and attractive to Ida and his group of inveterate problem solvers. Their focus on the problem of the stereo Pressman blinded them to the solution—to a different problem—that was in their hands.

"And then one day," said Takichi Tezuka, manager of product planning for the Tape Recorder Division, "into our room came Mr. Ibuka, our honorary chairman. He just popped into the room, saw us listening to this, and thought it was very interesting."

It is the province of honorary chairmen everywhere, because their status is almost invariably ceremonial, to putter about the plant looking in on this group and that group, nodding over the latest incomprehensible gadget. To this mundane task, Masaru Ibuka brought an undiminished intelligence and an active imagination. When he happened into the Tape Recorder Division and saw Ida's incomplete tape recorder, he admired the quality of its stereophonic sound. He also remembered an entirely unrelated project going on elsewhere in the building, where an engineer named Yoshiyuki Kamon was working to develop lightweight portable headphones.

What if you combined them? asked Ibuka. At the very least, he said, the headphones would use battery power much more efficiently than stereo speakers. Reduce power requirements and you can reduce battery consumption. But another idea began to form in his mind. If you added the headphones, wouldn't you dramatically increase the quality of what the listener hears? Could you leave out the recorder entirely and make a successful product that just plays music?

In the world of tape recorders, Ibuka's thought was heresy. He was mixing up functions. Headphones traditionally were supposed to extend the usefulness of tape recorders, not be essential to their success. This idea was so well established that if Ibuka had not made an association between a defective tape recorder design and the unfinished headphone design, Walkman may well have remained a little byway in musical history. Design groups within Sony tend to be very close-knit and remain focused on short-term task completion. Even when things were less busy, there was no reason for tape recorder people ever to communicate with headphone people. They had nothing to do with each other. Tezuka, the man who later was described as "the secretariat of the Walkman project," said, "No one dreamed that a headphone would ever come in a package with a tape recorder. We're not very interested in what they do in the Headphone Division."

But, even without this insularity, there is no assurance that someone else at Sony would have made the connection that Ibuka made. To people today, the relationship between a cassette player and a set of headphones is self-evident. But to people at Sony, and at virtually every consumer electronics company, that connection was invisible in 1978.

Ibuka got a predictable response from the researchers in the electronics lab and from others in the Tape Recorder and Headphone divisions. They were painfully polite but noncommittal. Ibuka might be right that the headphones would improve Pressman's efficiency, but nobody could guess how much of an improvement that would be. No one wanted to tell Ibuka that the idea of removing the speaker in favor of headphones was crazy. But it was! What if the owner of the device wanted to play back a tape so that more than one person could listen?

When Ibuka ventured further into illogic by suggesting a playback machine with *no speaker* and *no recorder,* he lost everybody. Who would want to buy such a thing? Who in Sony Corporation would support even ten minutes of development on such a harebrained scheme?

In a way, they were right and Ibuka was wrong. This was an idea that violated most industries' well-established criteria for judging the natural increments of product development. It only makes sense that a new product prototype should be better than the previous generation of product. Ida's nonrecording prototype seemed *worse*. The idea had no support from the people who eventually would be responsible for funding its development, carrying out the research, and trying to sell it to a consumer market. The idea should have been killed. The system made sense and the people who worked within the system were making sense.

For Honorary Chairman Ibuka, the handwriting was on the wall. Even though he was a revered man at Sony, he had no authority to order such a project undertaken against the wishes of the division's leaders. It was clear that the only way to sell a bad idea to a group of cautious, reasonable businessmen was to find an ally. So, in his enthusiasm, his next step was straight to the office of his partner and friend, Akio Morita.

SOURCE: Nayak & Ketteringham, 1986.

Discussion Questions

1. What principles of rational problem solving and creative problem solving were used in this case?
2. How was innovativeness fostered within Sony by top managers?
3. What roles were played by the various characters in the case that led to the success of the Walkman?
4. If you were a consultant to Sony, what would you advise to help foster this kind of innovation more frequently and more broadly throughout the company?

SKILL PRACTICE

EXERCISES FOR APPLYING CONCEPTUAL BLOCKBUSTING

Background

Creative problem solving is most applicable to problems that have no obvious solutions. Most problems people face can be solved relatively easily with a systematic analysis of alternatives. But other problems are ambiguous enough that obvious alternatives are not workable, and they require non-traditional approaches to find reasonable alternatives. The following is one such problem. It is real, not fictitious, and it probably characterizes your own college or university or public library. Apply the principles of creative problem solving in the chapter to come up with some realistic, cost-effective, creative solutions to this problem. Don't stop at the first solutions that come to mind, because there are no obvious right answers.

Assignment

Small groups should be formed to engage in the following problem-solving exercises. Each group should generate solutions to the cases. Each case is factual, not fictitious. Try to be as creative in your solutions as possible. The creativity of those solutions should be judged by an independent observer, and the best group's solution should be given recognition.

In defining and solving the problems, use the following five steps. Do not skip steps.

1. Generate a single statement that accurately defines the problem. Make sure that all group members agree with the definition of the problem.

2. Only after the problem statement has been written should you propose some alternative solutions to the problem. Write these down and be prepared to report them to the larger group.

3. All small groups should report their top three alternatives to the large group. The top three are the ones that most group members agree would produce the best solution to the problem.

4. Now, in the small group, generate at least five plausible alternative definitions of the problem. Use any of the techniques for expanding problem definition discussed in the text. Each problem statement should differ from the others in its definition, not just in its attributions or causes of the problem.

5. After the group has agreed on the wording of the five different statements, identify at least ten new alternatives for solving the problems you have defined in step 4. That is, apply the techniques for expanding alternatives discussed in the text.

As a result of steps 4 and 5, your group should have identified some new alternatives as well as more alternatives than you did in steps 1 and 2. Report to the large group the three alternatives that your small group judges to be the most creative.

An observer should provide feedback on the extent to which each group member applied these principles effectively, using the Observer's Feedback Form on page 86 in Appendix I.

The Bleak Future of Knowledge

Libraries throughout the world are charged with the responsibility of preserving the accumulated wisdom of the past and gathering information in the present.

They serve as sources of information and resources, alternate schools, and places of exploration and discovery. No one would question the value of libraries to societies and cultures throughout the world. The materials housed there are the very foundation of civilization. But consider the following two problems.

1. In America alone (and the problem is much worse in Eastern Europe and the former Soviet-bloc countries), hundreds of thousands of books are in states of decay so advanced that when they are touched they fall into powder. Whereas parchments seem to survive better when they are handled, and books printed before 1830 on rag paper stay flexible and tough, books printed since the mid-nineteenth century on wood-pulp paper are being steadily eaten away by natural acids. At the Library of Congress, about 77,000 books out of the stock of 13 million enter the endangered category every year. Fairly soon, about 40 percent of the books in the biggest research collections in America will be too fragile to handle. At the Bibliothèque Nationale in France, more than 600,000 books require treatment immediately. The largest library in England, the British Library, has a backlog of 1.6 million urgent cases.

2. The Library of Congress estimates that it will take twenty-five years to work through the backlog of cases. But of more concern is the fact that it costs about $200 in time and labor to treat a single volume. It costs more if it is to be put on another medium such as microfiche. The budget for most large libraries in the U.S., including the Library of Congress, has been cut during the 1970s and 1980s, and with pressure to raise taxes to fund social programs ever present on a national level and the cost of higher education rising beyond the inflation rate in universities, it is doubtful that book preservation will receive high funding priority in the near future.

SOURCE: *The Economist*, December 23, 1989.

Keith Dunn and McGuffey's Restaurant

Keith Dunn knew exactly what to expect. He knew how his employees felt about him. That's why he had sent them the questionnaire in the first place. He needed a shot of confidence, a feeling that employees were behind him as he struggled to build McGuffey's Restaurants, Inc., beyond two restaurants and $4 million in annual sales.

Gathering up the anonymous questionnaires, Dunn returned to his tiny corporate office in Asheville, N.C. With one of his partners by his side, he ripped open the first envelope as eagerly as a Broadway producer checking the reviews on opening night. His eyes zoomed directly to the question where employees were asked to rate the three owners' performance on a scale of one to ten.

A zero. The employee had scrawled in a big, fat zero. "Find out whose handwriting this is," he told his partner, Richard Laibson.

He ripped open another: zero again. And another. A two. "We'll fire these people," Dunn said to Laibson coldly.

Another zero.

A one.

"Oh, go work for somebody else, you jerk!" Dunn shouted.

Soon he had moved to fire ten of his 230 employees. "Plenty of people seemed to hate my guts," he says.

Over the next day, though, Dunn's anger subsided. "You think, 'I've done all this for these people and they think I'm a total jerk who doesn't care about them,'" he says. "Finally, you have to look in the mirror and think, 'Maybe they're right.'"

For Dunn, that realization was absolutely shattering. He had started the company three years earlier, in 1983, out of frustration over all the abuse *he* had suffered while working at big restaurant chains. If Dunn had one overriding mission at McGuffey's, it was to prove that restaurants didn't have to mistreat their employees.

He thought he had succeeded. Until he opened those surveys, he had believed McGuffey's was a place where employees felt valued, involved, and appreciated. "I had no idea we were treating people so badly," he says. Somewhere along the way, in the day-to-day running of the business, he had lost his connection with them and left behind the employee-oriented company he thought he was running.

Dunn's thirteen-year odyssey through some big restaurant chains left him feeling as limp as a cheeseburger after a day under the heat lamps. Ponderosa in Georgia. Bennigan's in Florida and Tennessee. TGI Friday's in Texas, Tennessee, and Indiana. Within one six-month period at Friday's, he got two promotions, two bonuses, and two raises—then his boss left, and he got fired. That did it. Dunn was fed up with big chains.

In 1982, at twenty-nine, he returned to Atlanta, where he had attended Emory University as an undergraduate, and began waiting tables at a local restaurant.

There he met David Lynn, the general manager of the restaurant, a similarly jaded twenty-nine-year-old who, by his own admission, had "begun to lose faith." Lynn and Dunn started hatching plans to open their own place, where employees would enjoy working as much as customers enjoyed eating. They planned to target the smaller markets that the chains ignored. With financing from a friend, they opened McGuffey's in 1983.

True to their people-oriented goals, the partners tried to make employees feel more appreciated than they themselves had felt at the chains. They gave them a free drink and a meal at the end of every shift, let them give away appetizers and desserts, and provided them a week of paid vacation each year.

A special camaraderie developed among the employees. After all, they worked in an industry in which a turnover rate of 250 percent was something to aspire to. The night before McGuffey's opened, in October 1983, some seventy-five employees encircled the ficus tree next to the bar, joined hands, and prayed silently for two minutes. "The tree had a special energy," says Dunn.

Maybe so. By the third night of operation, the 230-seat McGuffey's had a waiting list. The dining room was so crowded that after three months the owners decided to add a fifty-eight-seat patio. Then they had to rearrange the kitchen to handle the volume. In its first three and a half months, McGuffey's racked up sales of about $415,000, ending 1983 just over $110,000 in the red, mostly because the partners paid back the bulk of their $162,000 debt right away.

Word of the restaurant's success reached Hendersonville, N.C., a town of 30,000 about twenty miles away. The managing agent of a mall there—*the* mall there—even stopped by to recruit the partners. They made some audacious requests, asking him to spend $300,000 on renovations, including the addition of a patio and upgraded equipment. The agent agreed. With almost no market research, they opened the second McGuffey's in April, 1985; the first, in Asheville, was still roaring, having broken the $2 million mark in sales its first year, with a marginal loss of just over $16,000.

By midsummer, the 200-seat Hendersonville restaurant was hauling in $35,000 a week. "Gee, you guys must be getting rich," the partners heard all around town, "When are you going to buy your own jets?" "Everyone was telling us we could do no wrong," says Dunn. The Asheville restaurant, though, was developing some problems. Right after the Hendersonville McGuffey's opened, sales at Asheville fell 15 percent. But the partners shrugged it off; some Asheville customers lived closer to Hendersonville, so one restaurant was probably pulling some of the other's customers. Either way, the customers were still there. "We're just spreading our market a little thinner," Dunn told his partners. When Asheville had lost another 10 percent and Hendersonville 5 percent, Dunn blamed the fact that the drinking age had been raised to twenty-one in Asheville, cutting into liquor sales.

By 1985 the company recorded nearly $3.5 million in sales, with nominal losses of about $95,000. But the adulation and the expectation of big money and fancy cars were beginning to cloud the real reason they had started the business. "McGuffey's was born purely out of frustration," says Dunn. Now, the frustration was gone. "You get pulled in so many directions that you just lose touch," says Brandson. "There are things that you simply forget."

What the partners forgot, in the warm flush of success, were their roots.

"Success breeds ego," says Dunn, "and ego breeds contempt." He would come back from trade shows or real-estate meetings all pumped up. "Isn't this exciting?" he'd ask an employee. "We're going to open a new restaurant next year." When the employee stared back blankly, Dunn felt resentful. "I didn't understand why they weren't thrilled," he says. He didn't see that while his world was constantly growing and expanding, his employees' world was sliding downhill. They were still busing tables or cooking burgers and thinking, "Forget the new restaurant; you haven't said hello to me in months; and by the way, why don't you fix the tea machine?"

"I just got too good, and too busy, to do orientation," he says. So he decided to tape orientation sessions for new employees, to make a film just like the one he had been subjected to when he worked at Bennigan's. On tape, Dunn told new employees one of his favorite stories, the one about the customer who walks into a chain restaurant and finds himself asking questions of a hostess sign because he can't find a human. The moral: "McGuffey's will never be so impersonal as to make people talk to a sign." A film maybe, but never a sign.

Since Dunn wasn't around the restaurants all that much, he didn't notice that employees were leaving in droves. Even the departure of Tom Valdez, the kitchen manager in Asheville, wasn't enough to take the shine off his "glowing ego," as he calls it.

Valdez had worked as Dunn's kitchen manager at TGI Friday's. When the Hendersonville McGuffey's was opening up, Dunn recruited him as kitchen manager. A few months later Valdez marched into Dunn's office and announced that he was heading back to Indianapolis. "There's too much b.s. around here," he blurted out. "You don't care about your people." Dunn was shocked. "As soon as we get this next restaurant opened, we'll make things the way they used to be," he replied. But Valdez wouldn't budge. "Keith," he said bitterly, "you are turning out to be like all the other companies." Dunn shrugged. "We're a big company, and we've got to do big-company things," he replied.

Valdez walked out, slamming the door. Dunn still didn't understand that he had begun imitating the very companies that he had so loathed. He stopped wanting to rebel against them; under the intense pressure of growing a company, he just wanted to master their tried-and-true methods. "I was allowing the company to become like the companies we hated because I thought it was inevitable," he says.

Three months later McGuffey's two top managers announced that they were moving to the West Coast to start their own company. Dunn beamed, "Our employees learn so much," he would boast, "that they are ready to start their own restaurants."

Before they left Dunn sat down with them in the classroom at Hendersonville. "So," he asked casually, "how do you think we could run the place better?" Three hours later he was still listening. "The McGuffey's we fell in love with just doesn't exist anymore," one of them concluded sadly.

Dunn was outraged. How could his employees be so ungrateful? Couldn't they see how everybody was sharing the success? Who had given them health insurance as soon as the partners could afford it? Who had given them dental insurance this year? And who—not that anyone would appreciate it—planned to set up profit sharing next year?

Sales at both restaurants were still dwindling. This time, there were no changes in the liquor laws or new restaurants to blame. With employees feeling ignored, resentful, and abandoned, the rest rooms didn't get scrubbed as thoroughly, the food didn't arrive quite as piping hot, the servers didn't smile so often. But the owners, wrapped up in themselves, couldn't see it. They were mystified. "It began to seem like what made our company great had somehow gotten lost," says Brandson.

Shaken by all the recent defections, Dunn needed a boost of confidence. So he sent out the one-page survey, which asked employees to rate the owners' performance. He was crushed by the results. Out of curiosity, Dunn later turned to an assistant and asked a favor. Can you calculate our turnover rate? Came the reply: 220 percent, sir.

Keith Dunn figured he would consult the management gurus through their books, tapes, and speeches. You want people-oriented management, he thought, fine. I'll give it to you.

Dunn and Laibson had spent a few months visiting twenty-three of the best restaurants in the Southeast. Driving for hours, they'd listen to tapes on management, stop them at key points, and ask, "Why don't we do something like this?" At night, they read management books, underlining significant passages, looking for answers.

"They were all saying that people is where it's at," says Dunn. We've got to start thinking of our people as an asset, they decided. And we've got to increase the value of that asset. Dunn was excited by the prospect of forming McGuffey's into the shape of a reverse pyramid, with employees on top. Keeping employees, he now knew, meant keeping employees involved.

He heard consultant Don Beveridge suggest that smart companies kept managers involved by tieing their compensation to their performance. McGuffey's had been handing managers goals every quarter; if they hit half the goals, they pocketed half their bonus. Sound reasonable? No, preached Beveridge, you can't reward managers for a halfhearted job. It has to be all or nothing. "From now on," Dunn told his managers firmly, "there's no halfway."

Dunn also launched a contest for employees. Competition, he had read, was a good way of keeping employees motivated.

So the CUDA (Customer Undeniably Deserves Attention) contest was born. At Hendersonville and Asheville, he divided the employees into six teams. The winning team would win $1,000, based on talking to customers, keeping the restaurant clean, and collecting special tokens for extra work beyond the call of duty.

Employees came in every morning, donned their colors, and dug in for battle. Within a few weeks, two teams pulled out in front. Managers also seemed revitalized. To Dunn, it seemed like they would do anything, *anything,* to keep their food costs down, their sales up, their profit margins in line. This was just what Tom Peters, Kenneth Blanchard, Don Beveridge, Zig Ziglar, and the others had promised.

But after about six months, only one store's managers seemed capable of winning those all-or-nothing bonuses. At managers' meetings and reviews, Dunn started hearing grumblings. "How come your labor costs are so out of whack?" he'd ask. "Heck, I can't win the bonus anyway," a manager would answer, "so why try?" "Look, Keith," another would say, "I haven't seen a bonus in so long I've forgotten what they look like." Some managers wanted the bonus so badly that they worked understaffed, didn't fix equipment, and ran short on supplies.

The CUDA contest deteriorated into jealousy and malaise. Three teams lagged far behind after the first month or so. Within those teams people were bickering and complaining all the time. We can't win, so what's the use? The contest, Dunn couldn't help but notice, seemed to be having a reverse effect than the one he had intended. "Some people were really killing themselves," he says. About twelve, to be exact. The other 100-plus were utterly demoralized.

Dunn was angry. These were the same employees who, after all, had claimed he wasn't doing enough for them. But OK, he wanted to hear what they had to say. Get feedback, Tom Peters preached, find out what your employees think. Dunn announced that the owners would hold informal rap sessions once a month.

This is your time to talk, Dunn told the employees who showed up—all three of them. That's how it was most times, with three to five employees in attendance, and the owners dragging others away from their jobs in the kitchen. Nothing was sinking in, and Dunn knew it.

SOURCE: Adapted from Hyatt, 1989, p. 63–68.

SKILL APPLICATION

APPLICATION ACTIVITIES FOR SOLVING PROBLEMS CREATIVELY

Suggested Assignments

1. Teach someone else how to solve problems creatively. Record your experience in your journal.

2. Think of a problem that is important to you right now for which there is no obvious solution. Use the principles and techniques discussed in the module to work out a creative solution to that problem. Spend the time it takes to do a good job. (It may take several days or longer.) Describe the experience in your journal.

3. Help direct a group (your family, roommates, social club, church, or whatever) in a creative problem-solving exercise using techniques discussed in the module that seem to apply. Record your experience in your journal.

4. Write a letter to a congressional representative, dean, or CEO identifying several alternative solutions to some perplexing problem facing his or her organization, community, or state right now. Write about an issue that you care about. But do something different from most such letters: offer some suggestions for solution! This will require that you apply in advance the principles of problem solving discussed in the module.

Application Plan and Evaluation

The intent of this exercise is to help you apply this cluster of skills in a real-life, out-of-class setting. Now that you have become familiar with the behavioral guidelines that form the basis of effective skill performance, you will improve the most by trying out those guidelines in an everyday context. The trouble is, unlike a classroom activity in which feedback is immediate and others can assist you with their evaluations, this skill application activity is one you must accomplish and evaluate on your own. There are two parts to this activity. Part 1 helps prepare you to apply the skill. Part 2 helps you evaluate and improve on your experience. Be sure to actually write down answers to each item. Don't short-circuit the process by skipping steps.

Part 1—Planning

1. Write down the two or three aspects of this skill that are most important to you. These may be areas of weakness, areas you most want to improve, or areas that are most salient to a problem you face right now. Identify the specific aspects of this skill that you want to apply.

   _____

   _____

   _____

   _____

   _____

   _____

2. Now identify the setting or the situation in which you will apply this skill. Establish a plan for performance by actually writing down the situation. Who else will be involved? When will you do it? Where will it be done?

   Circumstances: _____

   Who else? _____

   When? _____

   Where? _____

3. Identify the specific behaviors you will engage in to apply this skill. Operationalize your skill performance.

   _____

   _____

   _____

   _____

   _____

4. What are the indicators of successful performance? How will you know you have succeeded in being effective? What will indicate you have performed competently?

   _____

   _____

   _____

   _____

   _____

   _____

Part 2—Evaluation

5. After you have completed your implementation, record the results. What happened? How successful were you? What was the effect on others?

_____

_____

_____

_____

_____

6. How can you improve? What modifications can you make next time? What will you do differently in a similar situation in the future?

_____

_____

_____

_____

_____

7. Looking back on your whole skill practice and application experience, what have you learned? What has been surprising? In what ways might this experience help you in the long term?

_____

_____

_____

_____

_____

APPENDIXES

SCORING KEYS AND SUPPLEMENTAL MATERIALS

SCORING KEY

Creative Problem Solving (page 20)

SKILL AREA	ITEMS	ASSESSMENT PRE-	POST-
Rational Problem Solving	1, 2, 3, 4, 5	_____	_____
Creative Problem Solving	6, 7, 8, 9, 10, 11, 12, 13, 14, 15	_____	_____
Fostering Innovation	16, 17, 18, 19, 20, 21, 22	_____	_____
TOTAL SCORE		_____	_____

To assess how well you scored on this instrument, compare your scores to three comparison standards: (1) Compare your score against the maximum possible (132). (2) Compare your scores with the scores of other students in your class. (3) Compare your scores to a norm group consisting of 500 business school students. In comparison to the norm group, if you scored

105 or above, you are in the top quartile.
94 to 104, you are in the second quartile.
83 to 93, you are in the third quartile.
82 or below, you are in the bottom quartile.

SCORING KEY

How Creative Are You? (page 22)

To compute your score, circle and add up the values assigned to each item. The values are as follows:

	A Agree	B Undecided or Don't Know	C Disagree		A Agree	B Undecided or Don't Know	C Disagree
1.	0	1	2	10.	1	0	3
2.	0	1	2	11.	4	1	0
3.	4	1	0	12.	3	0	−1
4.	−2	0	3	13.	2	1	0
5.	2	1	0	14.	4	0	−2
6.	−1	0	3	15.	−1	0	2
7.	3	0	−1	16.	2	1	0
8.	0	1	2	17.	0	1	2
9.	3	0	−1	18.	3	0	−1

	A Agree	B Undecided or Don't Know	C Disagree		A Agree	B Undecided or Don't Know	C Disagree
19.	0	1	2	30.	−2	0	3
20.	0	1	2	31.	0	1	2
21.	0	1	2	32.	0	1	2
22.	3	0	−1	33.	3	0	−1
23.	0	1	2	34.	−1	0	2
24.	−1	0	2	35.	0	1	2
25.	0	1	3	36.	1	2	3
26.	−1	0	2	37.	2	1	0
27.	2	1	0	38.	0	1	2
28.	2	0	−1	39.	−1	0	2
29.	0	1	2				

40. The following have values of 2:

energetic	dynamic	perceptive	dedicated
resourceful	flexible	innovative	courageous
original	observant	self-demanding	curious
enthusiastic	independent	persevering	involved

The following have values of 1:

self-confident	determined	informal	forward-looking
thorough	restless	alert	open-minded

The rest have values of 0.

TOTAL SCORE

95–116	Exceptionally creative
65–94	Very creative
40–64	Above average
20–39	Average
10–19	Below average
Below 10	Noncreative

SCORING KEY

Innovative Attitude Scale (page 24)

To determine your score for the Innovative Attitude Scale, simply add up the numbers associated with your responses to the twenty items. When you have done so, compare that score to the following norm group (consisting of graduate and undergraduate business school students, all of whom were employed full time).

Score	Percentile*
39	5
53	16
62	33
71	50
80	68
89	86
97	95

*Percentile indicates the percent of the people who are expected to score below you.

OBSERVER'S FEEDBACK FORM

Applying Conceptual Blockbusting

The Bleak Future of Knowledge (page 74)
Keith Dunn and McGuffey's Restaurant (page 75)

After the group has completed its problem-solving task, take the time to give the group feedback on its performance. Also provide feedback to each individual group member, either by means of written notes or verbal comments.

Group Observation

1. Was the problem defined explicitly?
    a. To what extent was information sought from all group members?
    b. Did the group avoid defining the problem as a disguised solution?
    c. What techniques were used to expand or alter the definitions of the problem?

_____

_____

_____

2. Were alternatives proposed before any solution was evaluated?
   a. Did all group members help generate alternative solutions without judging them one at a time?
   b. Did people build on the alternatives proposed by others?
   c. What techniques were used to generate more creative alternatives for solving the problem?

   _____

   _____

   _____

   _____

3. Was the optimal solution selected?
   a. Were alternatives evaluated systematically?
   b. Was consideration given to the realistic long-term effects of each alternative?

   _____

   _____

   _____

   _____

4. Was consideration given to how and when the solution could be implemented?
   a. Were obstacles to implementation discussed?
   b. Was the solution accepted because it solved the problem under consideration, or for some other reason?

   _____

   _____

   _____

   _____

5. How creative was the group in defining and solving the problem?

   _____

   _____

   _____

   _____

6. What techniques of conceptual blockbusting did the group use?

   _____

   _____

   _____

   _____

Individual Observation

1. What violations of the rational problem-solving process did you observe in this person?

_____

_____

_____

_____

2. What conceptual blocks were evident in this person?

_____

_____

_____

_____

3. What conceptual blockbusting efforts did this person make?

_____

_____

_____

_____

4. What was especially effective about the problem-solving attempts of this person?

_____

_____

_____

_____

5. What could this individual do to improve problem-solving skills?

_____

_____

_____

_____

Answers and Solutions to Problems

Page 39.   Solution to the Roman numeral problem.

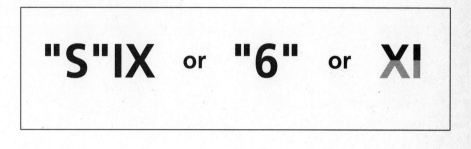

Page 39.   Solution to the matchstick problem in Figure 1.

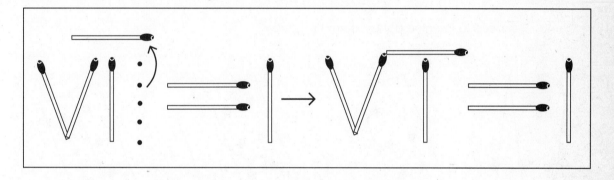

Page 41.   Answer to the Shakespeare problem in Figure 2:
5 inches. (Be careful to note where page 1 of Volume 1 is and where the last page of Volume 4 is.)

Page 42.   Common terms applying to both water and finance:

banks	deposits	capital drain
currency	frozen assets	sinking fund
cash flow	float a loan	liquid assets
washed up	underwater pricing	slush fund

Page 42.   Answer to the Descartes story: At the foundation of Descartes' philosophy was the statement, "I think, therefore I am."

Page 42.   Solution to the block of wood problem in Figure 3.

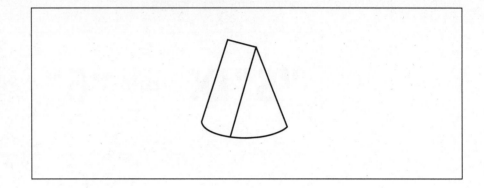

Page 43.   Solutions to the nine-dot problem in Figure 4.

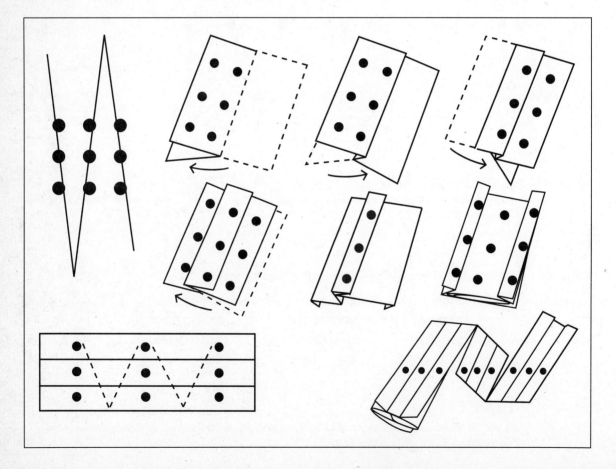

Page 45.   Solutions to embedded-patterns problem in Figure 5.

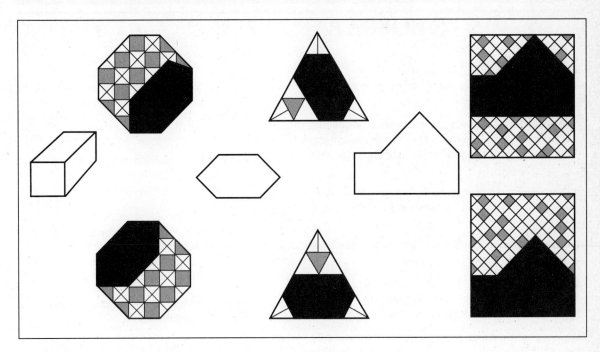

Page 57.   Solution to the fractionation problem in Figure 7.

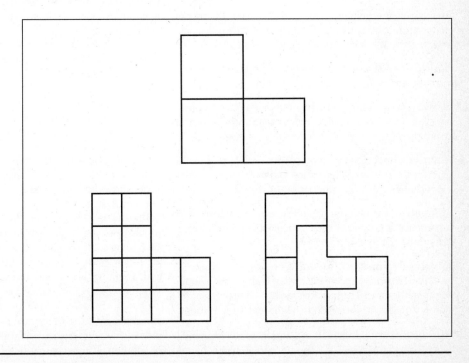

GLOSSARY

ability: the product of aptitude multiplied by training and opportunity.

accommodating approach: a response to conflict that tries to preserve a friendly interpersonal relationship by satisfying the other party's concerns while ignoring one's own. It generally ends with both parties losing.

accurate feedback: honest and open appraisal of subordinates' performance that is essential to an effective motivational program.

advising response: a response that provides direction, evaluation, personal opinion, or instructions.

altruistic-nurturing: a type of personality that seeks gratification through promoting harmony with others and enhancing their welfare without expectation of reward.

ambidextrous thinking: the use of both the left and right sides of the brain, indicative of the most creative problem solvers.

analytic-autonomizing: a type of personality that seeks gratification through the achievement of self-sufficiency, self-reliance, and logical orderliness.

anticipatory stressor: the anxious expectation of unfamiliar, uncertain, or disagreeable events.

artificial constraints: arbitrary boundaries placed around a problem that restrict possible alternative approaches and make the problem impossible to solve creatively.

assertive-directing: the type of personality that seeks gratification through self-assertion and directing the activities of others with the expectation of reward.

autonomy: the freedom to choose how and when to do a particular task; one of the characteristics of an intrinsically satisfying job.

avoiding response: an unassertive, uncooperative reaction to conflict that neglects the interests of both parties by side-stepping the issue. The resulting frustration may engender power struggles as others rush to fill the leadership vacuum.

bias against thinking: the inclination to avoid mental work, one indication of the conceptual block, complacency.

bipolar question: a poorly constructed interview question that gives interviewees only two limited options to choose from in answering. The result may be inaccurate information.

brainstorming: a technique designed to help people solve problems by generating alternative solutions without prematurely evaluating and rejecting them.

centrality: the attribute of a position in which the occupant is a key member of informal networks of task-related and interpersonal relationships. The resulting access to information, resources, and the personal commitment of others is an important source of power.

clarification probe: question(s) designed to clarify information given by the interviewee.

closed questions: interview questions designed to elicit specific information from interviewees by restricting the possible answers the interviewee can give. Useful when time is limited and/or when answers to open questions need clarifying.

coaching: interpersonal communication used by managers to pass along advice and information or to set standards for subordinates.

cognitive style: the manner in which an individual gathers and evaluates information he/she receives.

cognitive style strategies: particular problem-solving patterns established in individuals by the way they take in, code, and store information.

collaborating response: the cooperative, assertive, problem-solving mode of responding to conflict. It focuses on finding solutions to the basic problems and issues that are acceptable to both parties rather than on finding fault and assigning blame. Of the conflict-management approaches, this is the only win-win strategy.

commitment: the conceptual block that results when an individual endorses a particular point of view, definition, or solution. It is likely that he or she will follow through on that commitment.

competition-cooperation: studies consistently show that groups whose members are working toward a common goal perform more effectively and produce higher levels of member satisfaction than groups whose members seek to fulfill individual needs or pursue competing goals.

complacency: the conceptual block that occurs not because of poor thinking habits or inappropriate assumptions but because of fear, ignorance, self-satisfaction, or mental laziness.

compression: the conceptual block that results from an individual's looking at a problem too narrowly, screening out too much relevant data, or making assumptions that inhibit solving the problem.

compromising response: a reaction to conflict that attempts to find satisfaction for both parties by "splitting the difference." If overused, it sends the message that settling disputes is more important than solving problems.

conceptual blocks: mental obstacles that restrict the way a problem is defined and limit the number of alternative solutions that might otherwise be considered.

conformity level: the second level of values maturity, at which moral reasoning is based on agreement with and support of society's conventions and expectations.

congruence: matching of a response, verbally and nonverbally, to the communication of what an individual is thinking and feeling.

conjunctive communication: connection of responses to previous messages in such a way that conversation flows smoothly.

constancy: the conceptual block that results from using only one way to look at a problem—to approach, define, describe, or solve it.

counseling: interpersonal communication used to help subordinates recognize their own problems rather than offering advice, direction, or a right answer.

criticality: the attribute of a position that makes it uniquely valuable to an organization. Such a position usually guarantees power to the occupant since it involves specific, highly technical tasks that cannot be shared or delegated.

deep relaxation: an approach for use in building psychological resiliency in which both body and mind become completely relaxed.

defensiveness: focusing on self-defense rather than listening; occurs when an individual feels threatened or punished by the communication.

deflecting response: a response that switches the focus from the communicator's subject to one selected by the listener; or simply the change of subject by the listener.

delegation: assignment of responsibility for tasks to subordinates.

descriptive communication: objective description of the event or behavior that needs modification; description of the reaction to the behavior or its consequences; and suggestion of a more acceptable alternative.

dignity (and liberty): the ethical decision principle that a decision is right and proper if it preserves the basic humanity of individuals and provides the opportunity for them to have greater freedom.

direct analogies: a synectic problem-solving technique in which individuals apply facts, technology, and previous experience to solving a problem.

disciplining: a motivational strategy by which a manager reacts negatively to an employee's undesirable behavior in order to discourage further occurrences. Disciplining may be useful up to a point but does not encourage exceptional performance.

disconfirmation: a "put-down"; or the feeling resulting from communication that demeans or belittles the recipient and threatens his or her sense of self-worth.

disjunctive communication: responses that are disconnected from what was stated before. It can result from (1) a lack of equal opportunity to speak; (2) long pauses in a speech or before a response; or (3) when one person decides the topic of conversation.

disowned communication: attribution to an unknown person, group, or some external source; allows the communicator to avoid responsibility for the message and therefore avoid investing in the interaction.

distributive approach: negotiation tactic that requires both parties to sacrifice something to resolve the conflict—to divide up a "fixed pie." (Contrast with the integrative approach.)

distributive justice: the ethical decision principle that a decision is right and proper if it benefits the least advantaged individuals.

dominant personality characteristics: those aspects of an individual's personality, such as altruism, assertiveness, and analyzing, that determine the type of conflict-handling strategy he or she prefers. The most effective managers use a variety of styles, tailoring their response to the situation.

double-barreled question: a problematic question that actually consists of two questions that should be asked separately in order to avoid confusing the interviewee.

egalitarian communication: treating subordinates as worthwhile, competent, and insightful by emphasizing joint problem solving rather than projecting a superior position.

elaboration probe: question(s) designed to pursue a topic further when an interviewee has responded with superficial or inadequate information.

employment-selection interview: an interview designed to help current organizational members choose new members on the basis of experience, work skills, and personal suitability for the job.

empowerment: the use of acquired power to give others power in order to accomplish objectives; because it strikes a balance between lack of power and abuse of power, it is both enobling and enabling.

enactive strategy: a method of managing stress that creates a new environment by eliminating the stressors.

encounter stressor: the type of stressor that results from interpersonal conflict.

enigma of self-awareness: the problem inherent in learning about oneself. Although self-knowledge is a prerequisite for growth and improvement, it may also inhibit that growth and improvement because of the individual's fear of and resistance to self-revelation.

environmental stress: conflict-fostering tension induced by such organizational factors as budget-tightening or uncertainty caused by rapid, repeated change.

equity: workers' perceptions of the fairness of rewards based on the comparison of what they are getting out of the work relationship (outcomes) to what they are putting into it (input).

evaluative communication: a statement that makes a judgment or places a label on other individuals or on their behavior.

expertise: cognitive ability resulting from formal training and education or from on-the-job experience; an important source of power in a technological society.

external locus: the viewpoint of an individual who attributes the outcome of his/her actions to outside forces.

external motivators: rewards for performance that are controlled by someone other than the employee—usually the supervisor—such as appreciation, job security, or good working conditions. (Compare with internal motivators.)

extra effort: working extraordinarily hard, especially on behalf of superiors, can gain an individual more power in an organization than his or her position in the hierarchy warrants.

fantasy analogies: a synectic problem-solving technique in which individuals ask, "In my wildest dreams, how would I wish the problem to be resolved?"

feedback: information regularly received by individuals from superiors about their performance on a job. Knowledge of results permits workers to understand how their efforts have contributed to organizational goals.

feeling strategy: a method of interpreting and judging information subjectively or impressionistically rather than objectively; one which defines and redefines a problem on a trial-and-error basis.

flexibility: the freedom to exercise one's judgment—an important prerequisite for gaining power in a position—particularly in tasks that are high in variety and novelty.

flexibility of thought: the diversity of ideas or concepts generated.

flexible communication: the result of the willingness of the coach or counselor to accept the existence of additional data or other alternatives and to acknowledge that other individuals may be able to make significant contributions both to the problem solution and to the relationship.

fluency of thought: the number of ideas or concepts produced in a given length of time.

forcing response: an assertive, uncooperative response to conflict that uses the exercise of authority to satisfy one's own needs at the expense of another's.

funnel sequence: a sequence of interview questions that begins with general questions and moves toward more and more specific questions.

goal characteristics: effective goals are specific, consistent, and appropriately challenging.

goal setting: the foundation of an effective motivational program, which consists of (1) including employees in the goal-setting process; (2) setting specific, consistent, and challenging goals; and (3) providing feedback.

goal-setting process: the critical consideration is that goals must be understood and accepted if they are to be effective.

group shift: the polarization effect that occurs during intensive group discussions as individuals tend to adopt a more extreme version of the position they held at the beginning of the meeting. The tendency is usually toward a risk-taking rather than a conservative stance.

groupthink: one of the pitfalls in group decision making that occurs when the pressure to reach consensus interferes with critical thinking. When the leader or the majority appears to prefer a particular solution, holders of dissenting views are reluctant to speak out.

hardiness: a combination of the three characteristics of a highly stress-resistant personality – control, commitment, and challenge.

homogeneity-heterogeneity: members of a homogeneous group share similar backgrounds, personalities, knowledge, and values. Due to this sameness, these groups tend to produce mundane and unimaginative outcomes. Members of a heterogeneous group are dissimilar and because of their differences are apt to be better at addressing novel, complex tasks.

idea champion: person who comes up with the innovative solutions to problems.

ignoring: a manager's neglect of both the performance and the satisfaction of employees. Such a lack of effective leadership can paralyze a work unit.

ignoring commonalities: a manifestation of the commitment block – the failure to identify similarities among seemingly disparate situations or data.

illumination stage: in creative thought, the third stage, which occurs when an insight is recognized and a creative solution is articulated.

imperviousness in communication: the failure of the communicator to acknowledge the feelings or opinions of the listener.

imposing: a manager's exploitation of employees by assigning tasks with the sole emphasis on performance and without regard to their job satisfaction – usually disastrous in the long term.

incubation stage: an early stage in creative thought in which mostly unconscious mental activity combines unrelated thoughts in pursuit of a solution to a problem.

indulging: a manager's emphasis on employee satisfaction to the exclusion of employee performance; the resulting country-club atmosphere hinders productivity.

information deficiencies: breakdowns in interorganizational communication. Conflicts based on the resulting misunderstandings tend to be common but easy to resolve.

information-gathering interview: an interview used to gather facts about an issue or to help in a problem-solving situation. Unlike other interviews, the interviewer can choose the interviewee.

initiator role: the part played in a conflict management model by the individual who first registers a complaint with another person who is the "responder." (See Behavioral Guidelines, *Developing Management Skills: Managing Conflict*)

innovativeness: fostering new ideas among individuals by methods such as placing them in teams and separating them at least temporarily from the normal pressures of organizational life.

instrumental values: those values that prescribe desirable standards of conduct or methods to reach a goal.

integrating: a motivation strategy that emphasizes job performance and job satisfaction equally – a challenging strategy for a manager to implement, but one that can result in both high productivity and high morale of employees.

integrative approach: negotiation tactic in which the focus is on collaborative ways of "expanding the pie" by avoiding fixed, incompatible positions. (Contrast with distributive approach.)

interchange incompatibility: the inability of individuals to communicate effectively owing to their having different interpersonal needs.

internal locus: the viewpoint of an individual who attributes the success or failure of particular behavior to his/her own actions.

internal motivators: job characteristics over which the manager has no control and that determine whether or not a particular employee will find that job interesting and satisfying. (Compare with external motivators.)

interpersonal compatibility: the matching of individuals' needs.

interpersonal competence: the ability to manage conflict, to build and manage high-performance teams, to conduct efficient meetings, to coach and counsel employees, to provide negative feedback in constructive ways, to influence others' opinions, and to motivate and energize employees.

interpersonal orientation: the aspect of self-awareness that relates to behavior and relationships with other people.

interview: a specialized form of communication conducted for a specific task-related purpose.

intuitive strategy: a type of thinking that uses preconceived notions about the sort of information that will be relevant and looks for commonalities among the various elements of data.

inverted funnel sequence: a sequence of interview questions that begins with specific questions and moves toward more and more general questions.

Janusian thinking: thinking contradictory thoughts at the same time; conceiving two opposing ideas to be true concurrently.

leading question: a tricky interview question that includes the desired answer in the question itself. While useful in a sales interview, it can lead to biased answers in other types of interviews.

left-hemisphere thinking: brain activity concerned with logical, analytic, linear, or sequential tasks.

legitimacy: conformity with an organization's value system and practices, which increases one's acceptance and thus one's influence in that organization.

level of initiative: the extent to which a subordinate is expected to take a task. At least five levels can be identified: (1) wait to be told; (2) ask what to do; (3) recommend, then act; (4) report after acting; and (5) act independently.

life balance: the development of resiliency in all areas of one's life in order to handle stress that cannot be eliminated.

locus of control: the second dimension of orientation toward change; the viewpoint from which an individual judges the extent to which he/she controls his/her own destiny.

mediator role: the conflict-management role played by the third party who intervenes in a dispute between an "initiator" and a "responder." (See Behavioral Guidelines, *Developing Management Skills: Managing Conflict.*)

morphological forced connections: a technique to expand alternative solutions by forcing the integration of seemingly unrelated elements. The four steps are (1) writing down the problem; (2) listing its attributes; (3) listing alternatives to each attribute; and (4) combining different alternatives from the attributes list.

motivation: a combination of desire and commitment demonstrated by effort.

need for affection: the drive for close personal relationships with others while preserving one's separateness.

need for control: the desire to maintain for oneself a satisfactory balance of power and influence in relationships.

need for inclusion: the basic desire of people to maintain relationships and share activities with others.

negotiation strategies: tactics used in the bargaining phase of negotiation—collaborating, forcing, and accommodating—that are consistent with the related conflict management approaches and have about the same outcomes.

neutralizing unwanted influence attempts: techniques of resisting or counteracting the three principal influence strategies: retribution, reciprocity, and reason.

nominal group technique (NGT): a group decision-making technique; a highly structured form of brainstorming. In an NGT session, group members (1) individually write down as many alternative solutions to a problem as they can think of, (2) report their ideas, which are transcribed onto a flip-chart, (3) discuss the ideas briefly for clarification only, and (4) vote for the alternatives they prefer. The process is repeated until a consensus is reached.

non-inquisitiveness: the failure to ask questions, obtain information, or search for data; an example of the complacency block.

open questions: interview questions designed to elicit general information from interviewees—how they feel, what their priorities are, and how much they know about a topic. Useful for establishing rapport, they can be time consuming.

orchestrator: person who brings together cross-functional groups and necessary political support to facilitate implementation of a creative idea.

orientation toward change: an individual's adaptability to ever-increasing levels of ambiguity and turbulence.

originator incompatibility: the stalemate that occurs when either both people want to initiate in an area or neither does.

owned communication: statements for which a person takes responsibility, acknowledging that he or she is the source of the message; an indication of supportive communication.

perceptual stereotyping: defining a problem by using preconceptions based on past experience, thus preventing the problem from being viewed in novel ways.

performance: the product of ability multiplied by motivation.

performance-appraisal interview: an interview designed to evaluate the past performance of a member of the organization and provide that member a means of feedback for the purpose of improving job performance.

personal analogies: recommended as part of synectics, whereby individuals try to identify themselves as the problem, asking the question, "If *I* were the problem, what would I like? What would satisfy me?"

personal attraction: "likability" stemming from agreeable behavior and attractive physical appearance; a combination of behaviors normally associated with friendship that have been shown to contribute to managerial success.

personal differences: variations among individuals' values and needs that have been shaped by different socialization processes. Interpersonal conflicts stemming from such incompatibilities are the most difficult for a manager to resolve.

personal management interview: a regularly scheduled, one-on-one meeting between a manager and his or her subordinates.

personal morality: the ethical code that a decision is right and proper if it is consistent with a set of guidelines taught by a religious organization, family, etc.

personal values: an individual's standards that define what is good/bad, worthwhile/worthless, desirable/undesirable, true/false, moral/immoral.

preparation stage: a stage in creative thought that includes gathering data, defining the problem, generating alternatives, and consciously examining all available information.

principled level: the third and highest level of values maturity in which an individual judges right from wrong by following internalized principles developed from personal experience.

proactive strategy: a method of managing stress that initiates action in order to resist the negative effects of stress.

probing response: a response that asks a question about what the communicator just said or about a topic selected by the listener.

rational problem solving: a method of solving problems that involves four steps: (1) defining the problem; (2) generating alternative solutions; (3) evaluating and selecting an alternative; and (4) implementing and following up on the solution.

reactive strategy: a method for managing stress that copes with the stressors immediately, temporarily reducing their effects.

reason: the influence strategy that relies on persuasion and appeal to rational consideration of the inherent merits of the request in order to gain compliance. It is explicit and direct, not manipulative.

reassigning: moving a poor performer to a position more consonant with his or her skill level and aptitude.

reciprocal incompatibility: the stalemate that occurs when there is no match between one person's expressed behavior and another's wanted behavior.

reciprocity: an influence strategy through which a manager uses bargaining as a tool for exacting a subordinate's compliance. This approach operates on the principle of self-interest and respect for the value of the interpersonal relationship.

redirection: a behavior-shaping process that follows a reprimand and gives the offender the opportunity to receive a future reward by modifying his or her behavior.

refitting: adapting the requirements of a job to an employee's abilities in order to improve poor performance.

reflecting response: a response that serves two purposes: (1) to confirm a message that was heard and (2) to communicate understanding and acceptance of the other person.

reflective probe: nondirective question(s) used for either elaboration or clarification of information; it generally mirrors or repeats some aspect of the interviewee's last answer.

relational algorithm: a blockbusting technique for combining unrelated attributes in problem solving by connecting words to force a relationship between two elements in a problem.

releasing: the last management option for solving a problem of poor performance—termination of employment.

relevance: the characteristic of a position whose tasks relate most closely to the dominant competitive goals of an organization and therefore enhance the power of the occupant.

repetition probe: a repeated or paraphrased question used if the interviewee has not directly answered a question the first time.

reprimand: a behavior-shaping approach used to transform unacceptable behaviors into acceptable ones; the discipline should be prompt and it should focus on the specific behavior.

resiliency: one's capacity to cope with stress.

responder role: the part played in a conflict-management model by the person who is supposedly the source of the "initiator's" problem. (See Behavioral Guidelines, *Developing Management Skills: Managing Conflict.*)

resupplying: managerial option for overcoming an employee's lack-of-ability problem that focuses on supplying the support needed to do the job.

retraining: a management tool for overcoming the problem of an employee's poor performance, especially needed in rapidly changing technical work environments.

retribution: an influence strategy that involves a threat—the denial of expected rewards or the imposition of punishment. It usually triggers an aversive response in the subordinate and the breakdown of the interpersonal relationship.

reversibility: the ethical decision principle that a decision is right and proper if the individual making the decision would be willing to be treated in the same way.

reverse the definition: a tool for improving and expanding problem definition by reversing the way you think of the problem.

rewarding: the motivational strategy that links desired behaviors with employee-valued outcomes. Such positive reinforcement gives an employee more incentive for exceptional accomplishment than does disciplining.

right-hemisphere thinking: mental activity concerned with intuition, synthesis, playfulness, and qualitative judgment.

rigidity in communication: a type of message that portrays the communication as absolute, unequivocal, or unquestionable.

role incompatibility: the conflict-producing difference between workers whose tasks are interdependent but whose priorities differ because their responsibilities within the organization differ. The mediation of a common superior is usually the best solution.

rule breaker: person who goes beyond organizational boundaries and barriers to ensure the success of an innovation.

self-awareness: a knowledge of one's own personality and individuality.

self-centered level: the first level of values maturity. It contains two stages of values development, moral reasoning and instrumental values, which are based on personal needs or wants and the consequences of an act.

self-disclosure: the revealing to others of ambiguous or inconsistent aspects of oneself, a process necessary for growth.

sensing strategy: a method of interpreting and judging information that is rational; it uses few preconceptions about what may be relevant and therefore examines the information closely and thoroughly, looking for uniqueness.

sensitive line: an invisible boundary around one's self-image, which, if threatened, will evoke a strong defensive reaction.

separating figure from ground: the ability to filter out inaccurate, misleading, or irrelevant information so a problem can be defined accurately and alternative solutions can be generated.

situational stressor: the type of stressor that arises from an individual's environment or circumstances, such as unfavorable working conditions.

skill variety: an attribute of a job that uses an individual's talents and abilities to the maximum and thus makes the job seem worthwhile and important.

small-wins strategy: a strategy for individuals to use for coping with stress; it involves celebrating each small successful step in the attack on a large project.

social loafing: a pitfall in group decision-making performance that occurs when the effort of a large group seems to negate the importance of each member's individual contribution. The result is that each member puts out less than his or her best effort. A group leader can counteract this tendency by emphasizing the importance of individual effort and by expressing positive expectations.

sponsor: person who helps provide the resources, environment, and encouragement that the idea champion needs in order to work.

stressors: stimuli that cause physiological and psychological reactions in individuals.

subdivision: the breaking apart of a problem into smaller parts.

superiority-oriented communication: a message that gives the impression that the communicator is informed while others are ignorant, adequate while others are inadequate, competent while others are incompetent, or powerful while others are impotent.

supportive communication: communication that helps managers share information accurately and honestly without jeopardizing interpersonal relationships.

symbolic analogies: symbols or images that are imposed on the problem; recommended as part of synectics.

synectics: a technique for improving creative problem solving by putting something you don't know in terms of something you do know.

task identity: an attribute of a job that enables an individual to perform a complete job from beginning to end.

task-process: research indicates that effective groups contain members who are highly task oriented as well as those who are concerned about maintaining the quality of the group's process. Task-oriented members are all business, focusing on outcomes and not worrying about members' feelings and attitudes; process-oriented members encourage everyone to participate and are most concerned with member satisfaction.

task significance: the degree to which the performance of a task affects the work or lives of other people. The greater its significance, the more meaningful the job is to the worker.

terminal values: those values that designate desirable ends or goals for an individual.

thinking languages: the various ways in which a problem can be considered, from verbal to nonverbal or symbolic languages as well as through sensory and visual imagery. Using only one thinking language is one indication of the constancy block.

thinking strategy: a method of interpreting and judging information in which an individual follows a systematic plan with specific sequential steps.

timely rewards: immediate and spontaneous feedback for desired behavior—important for an effective motivational program.

time stressor: the type of stressor generally caused by having too much to do in too little time.

tolerance of ambiguity: an individual's ability to cope with ambiguous, fast-changing, or unpredictable situations in which information is incomplete, unclear, or complex.

Type A personality: a hard-driving, hostile, intense, highly competitive personality.

universalism: the ethical decision principle that a decision is right and proper if everyone would be expected to behave in the same way under the same circumstances.

utilitarianism: the ethical decision principle that a decision is right and proper if it generates the greatest amount of good for the most people while producing no harm.

validating communication: a message that helps people feel recognized, understood, accepted and valued. It is egalitarian, flexible, two-way, and based on agreement.

verification stage: the final stage in creative thought in which the creative solution is evaluated relative to some standard of acceptability.

vertical thinking: defining a problem in a single way and then pursuing that definition without deviation until a solution is reached.

visibility: the power-enhancing attribute of a position that can usually be measured by the number of influential people one interacts with in the organization.

REFERENCES

Introduction

AACSB. *Preliminary report on the future of business education and development.* St. Louis, Mo., 1985.

Bandura, A. *A social learning theory.* Englewood Cliffs, N.J.: Prentice-Hall, 1977.

Behrman, Jack N., & Levin, Richard I. Are business schools doing their job? *Harvard Business Review,* 1983, *62,* 140–147.

Benson, Gary. On the campus: How well do business schools prepare graduates for the business world? *Personnel,* 1983, *60,* 61–65.

Boyatzis, Richard E. *The competent manager.* New York: Wiley, 1982.

Burnaska, R. F. The effects of behavioral modeling training upon managers' behavior and employees' perceptions. *Personnel Psychology,* 1976, *29,* 329–335.

Cameron, Kim S., & Whetten, David A. A model for teaching management skills. *Organizational Behavior Teaching Journal,* 1984, *8,* 21–27.

Cameron, Kim, & Tschirhart, Mary. *Managerial competencies and organizational effectiveness.* Working paper, School of Business Administration, University of Michigan, 1988.

Cheit, Earl F. Business schools and their critics. *California Management Review,* 1985, *27,* 43–62.

Cohen, Peter A. College grades and adult achievement: A research synthesis. *Research in Higher Education,* 1984, *20,* 281–291.

Controller of the Currency. *National bank failure.* U.S. Government Printing Office, 1987.

The crisis of business education. *New York Times,* August 25, 1983.

Curtis, Dan B., Winsor, Jerry L., & Stephens, Ronald D. National preferences in business and communication education. *Communication Education,* 1989, *38,* 6–15.

Davis, T. W., & Luthans, Fred. A social learning approach to organizational behavior. *Academy of Management Review,* 1980, *5,* 281–290.

Flanders, L. R. *Report 1 from the federal manager's job and role survey: Analysis of responses by SES and mid-management level executives and management development division.* U.S. Office of Personnel Management, Washington, D.C., 1981.

Ghiselli, E. E. Managerial talent. *American Psychologist,* 1963, *18,* 631–642.

Goldstein, A. P., & Sorcher, Melvin. *Changing supervisor behavior.* New York: Pergammon, 1974.

Hanson, Gary. *Determinants of firm performance: An integration of economic and organizational factors.* Unpublished doctoral dissertation, University of Michigan Business School, 1986.

Hayes, Robert H., & Abernathy, William. Managing our way to economic decline. *Harvard Business Review,* 1980, *59,* 66–77.

Holt, John. *How children fail.* New York: Pitman, 1964.

Hunsicker, Frank R. What successful managers say about their skills. *Personnel Journal,* 1978, November, 618–621.

Katz, Ralph L. Skills of an effective administrator. *Harvard Business Review,* 1974, *51,* 90–102.

Latham, G. P., & Saari, L. P. Application of social learning theory to training supervisors through behavioral modeling. *Journal of Applied Psychology,* 1979, *64,* 239–246.

Livingston, Sterling W. The myth of the well-educated manager. *Harvard Business Review,* 1971, *49,* 79–89.

Luthans, Fred, Rosenkrantz, Stuart A., & Hennessey, Harry W. What do successful managers really do? An observation study of managerial activities. *Journal of Applied Behavioral Science,* 1985, *21,* 255–270.

Mandt, Edward. The failure of business education. *Management Review,* 1982, August, 47–52.

Margerison, Charles, & Kakabadse, Andrew. *How American chief executives succeed.* New York: AMA Publications, 1984.

Miner, John B. The real crunch in managerial manpower. *Harvard Business Review,* 1973, *51,* 146–158.

Mintzberg, Henry. The manager's job: Folklore and fact. *Harvard Business Review,* 1975, *53,* 49–71.

Mintzberg, Henry. Training managers, not MBAs. Paper presented at the Macro Organizational Behavior Society meetings, Northwestern University, September 1987.

Moses, J. L., & Ritchie, R. J. Supervisory relationships training: A behavioral evaluation of a behavioral modeling program. *Personnel Psychology,* 1976, *29,* 337–343.

Overhauling America's business management. *New York Times,* May 24, 1981.

Peterson, Donald E. Personal communication, October 1990.

Peterson, Peter G. The morning after. *Atlantic Monthly,* October 1987, 43–69.

Peterson, Robert A., Kozmetsky, George, and Ridgeway, Nancy, M. Causes of small business failures. *American Journal of Small Business,* 1983, *8,* 15–19.

Pfeffer, Jeffrey. *Power in organizations.* Marshfield, Mass.: Pitman, 1981.

Pollock, Roy H. Cited in Peters, Thomas. *Thriving on chaos.* New York: Free Press, 1987.

Porras, J. I., & Anderson, B. Improving managerial effectiveness through modeling-based training. *Organizational Dynamics,* 1981, *9,* 60–77.

Porter, Lyman W., & McKibbin, Lawrence E. *Management education and development: Drift or thrust into the 21st century?* New York: McGraw-Hill, 1988.

Prentice, Marjorie G. An empirical search for a relevant management curriculum. *Collegiate News and Views,* 1984, Winter, 25–29.

Rose, S. D., Crayner, J. J., & Edleson, J. L. Measuring interpersonal competence. *Social Work,* 1977, *22,* 125–129.

Samuelson, Paul J. What good are B-schools? *Newsweek,* May 14, 1990, 49.

Schutz, W. C. *FIRO: A three-dimensional theory of interpersonal behavior.* New York: Holt, Rinehart & Winston, 1958.

Singleton, W. T., Spurgeon, P., & Stammers, R. B. *The analysis of social skill.* New York: Plenum, 1980.

Smith, P. E. Management modeling training to improve morale and customer satisfaction. *Personnel Psychology,* 1976, *29,* 351–359.

Staw, Barry M., Sandelands, Lance, & Dutton, Jane. Threat-rigidity effects in organizational behavior: A multilevel analysis. *Administrative Science Quarterly,* 1981, *26,* 501–524.

Steele, Jack. Personal communication, 1979.

Thurow, Lester C. *Dangerous currents.* New York: Random House, 1983.

Thurow, Lester C. Revitalizing American industry: Managing in a competitive world economy. *California Management Review,* 1984, *27,* 9–41.

Whetten, David A., & Cameron, Kim S. Management skill training: A needed addition to the management curriculum. *Organizational Behavior Teaching Journal,* 1983, *8,* 10–15.

Why businesses fail. Survey of 203 firms conducted by the Comprehensive Accounting Corporation, 1988.

Wrapp, H. Edward. Cited in Peters, Thomas J., & Waterman, Robert H. *In search of excellence.* New York: Harper & Row, 1982.

Solving Problems Creatively

Allen, J. L. *Conceptual blockbusting.* San Francisco: W. H. Freeman, 1974.

Amabile, Teresa M. A model of creativity and innovation in organizations. In Cummings, Larry L., & Staw, Barry M. (Eds.), *Research in organizational behavior,* 1988, *10,* 123–167.

Barron, F. X. *Creativity and psychological health.* New York: Van Nostrand, 1963.

Basadur, M. S. *Training in creative problem solving: Effects of deferred judgment and problem finding and solving in an industrial research organization.* Unpublished doctoral dissertation, University of Cincinnati, 1979.

Beveridge, W. *The art of scientific investigation.* New York: Random House, 1960.

Bower, M. Nurturing innovation in an organization. In G. A. Steiner (Ed.), *The creative organization.* Chicago: University of Chicago Press, 1965.

Broadwell, M. M. *The new supervisor.* Reading, Mass.: Addison-Wesley, 1972.

Bruner, J. S. *On knowing: Essays for the left hand.* Cambridge: Harvard University Press, 1966.

Cameron, K. S. Measuring organizational effectiveness in institutions of higher education. *Administrative Science Quarterly,* 1978, *23,* 604–632.

Campbell, N. *What is science?* New York: Dover, 1952.

Cialdini, Robert B. *Influence: Science and practice.* Glenview, Ill.: Scott, Foresman, 1988.

Crovitz, H. F. *Galton's walk.* New York: Harper & Row, 1970.

Dauw, D. C. *Creativity and innovation in organizations.* Dubuque, Iowa: Kendall Hunt, 1976.

deBono, E. *New think.* New York: Basic Books, 1968.

Dellas, M., & Gaier, E. L. Identification of creativity: The individual. *Psychological Bulletin,* 1970, *73,* 55–73.

Drath, W. H. Out of the blue. In *Issues and observations.* Greensboro, N.C.: Center for Creative Leadership, 1981.

Drucker, P. F. *Management.* New York: Harper & Row, 1974.

Einstein, A. *Fundamental ideas and methods of relativity theory, presented in their development.* (c. 1919, G. Holton). Unpublished manuscript.

Elbing, A. *Behavioral decisions in organizations.* Glenview, Ill.: Scott, Foresman, 1978.

Ettlie, John E., & O'Keefe, Robert D. Innovative attitudes, values, and intentions in organizations. *Journal of Management Studies,* 1982, *19,* 163–182.

Eysenck, H. *Know your own I.Q.* New York: Penguin, 1962.

Feldman, David. *Why do clocks run clockwise?* New York: National Syndications, 1988.

Festinger, Leon. *A theory of cognitive dissonance.* Stanford: Stanford University Press, 1957.

Filley, A. C., House, R. J., & Kerr, S. *Managerial process and organizational behavior.* Glenview, Ill.: Scott, Foresman, 1976.

Freedman, J. L., and Fraser, S. C. Compliance without pressure: The foot-in-the-door technique. *Journal of Personality and Social Psychology,* 1966, *4,* 195–202.

Galbraith, Jay R. Designing the innovating organization. *Organizational Dynamics,* 1982, Winter, 5–25.

Gardner, J. W. *Self-renewal.* New York: Harper & Row, 1965.

———. *The nature of human intelligence.* New York: McGraw-Hill, 1967.

Gordon, W. J. J. *Synectics: The development of creative capacity.* New York: Collier, 1961.

Guilford, J. P. Creativity: Its measurement and development. In S. J. Parnes & H. F. Harding (Eds.), *A sourcebook for creative thinking.* New York: Scribner, 1962.

Haefele, J. W. *Creativity and innovation.* New York: Reinhold, 1962.

Heider, Fritz. Attitudes and cognitive organization. *Journal of Psychology,* 1946, *21,* 107–112.

Hermann, N. The creative brain. *Training and Development Journal,* 1981.

Hermone, R. Creativity: The supervisor's secret. *Supervisory Management,* 1979, *29,* 24–28.

Huber, G. P. *Managerial decision making.* Glenview, Ill.: Scott, Foresman, 1980.

Hyatt, J. The odyssey of an excellent man. *Inc.,* 1989, February, 63–68.

Interaction Associates. *Tools for change.* San Francisco: Interaction Associates, 1971.

Janis, Irvin L. *Groupthink.* New York: Free Press, 1971.

Janis, I., & Mann, L. *Decision making.* New York: Free Press, 1977.

Kanter, Rosabeth M. *The change masters.* New York: Simon & Schuster, 1983.

Koberg, D., & Bagnall, J. *The universal traveler: A soft-system guidebook to creativity, problem solving, and the process of design.* Los Altos, Calif.: William Kaufmann, 1974.

Koestler, A. *The act of creation.* New York: Dell, 1967.

Leavitt, H. J. *Managerial psychology.* Chicago: University of Chicago Press, 1972.

Maier, N. R. F. Assets and liabilities of group problem solving: The need for an integrative function. *Psychological Review,* 1967, *74,* 239–249.

Maier, N. R. F. *Problem solving and creativity in individuals and groups.* Belmont, Calif.: Brooks/Cole, 1970.

March, J. G., & Simon, H. A. *Organizations.* New York: Wiley, 1958.

Markoff, John. For scientists using supercomputers, visual imagery speeds discoveries. New York Times News Service, *Ann Arbor News,* Nov. 2, 1988, D3.

Martindale, C. What makes creative people different. *Psychology Today,* 1975, *9,* 44–50.

Maslow, A. Emotional blocks to creativity. In S. J. Parnes & H. F. Harding (Eds.), *A sourcebook for creative thinking.* New York: Scribner, 1962.

McKim, R. H. *Experiences in visual thinking.* Monterey, Calif.: Brooks/Cole, 1972.

McMillan, Ian. *Progress in research on corporate venturing.* Working paper, Center for Entrepreneurial Studies, New York University, 1985.

Medawar, P. B. *The art of the soluable.* London: Methuen, 1967.

Mintzberg, H. *The nature of managerial work.* New York: Harper & Row, 1973.

Nayak, P. Ranganath, & Ketteringham, John M. *Breakthroughs!* New York: Rawson Associates, 1986.

Nemeth, C. J. Differential contributions of majority and minority influence. *Psychological Review,* 1986, *93,* 23–32.

Newcomb, Theodore. An approach to the study of communicative acts. *Psychological Review,* 1954, *60,* 393–404.

Olton, R., & Crutchfield, R. Developing the skills of productive thinking. Cited in R. H. McKim (Ed.) *Experiences in visual thinking.* Monterey, Calif.: Brooks/Cole, 1972.

Osborn, A. *Applied imagination.* New York: Scribner, 1953.

Parnes, S. J. Can creativity be increased? In S. J. Parnes & H. F. Harding (Eds.), *A sourcebook for creative thinking.* New York: Scribner, 1962.

Raudsepp, Eugene. *How Creative Are You?* New York: Putnam, 1981.

Raudsepp, E., & Hough, G. P., Jr. *Creative Growth Games.* New York: Putnam, 1977.

Rothenberg, A. Creative contradictions. *Psychology Today,* 1979, *13,* 55–62.

Rothenburg, A. *The emerging goddess.* Chicago: University of Chicago Press, 1979.

Schumacher, E. F. *A guide for the perplexed.* New York: Harper & Row, 1977.

Scott, Otto J. *The creative ordeal: The story of Raytheon.* New York: Atheneum, 1974.

Steiner, G. *The creative organization.* Chicago: University of Chicago Press, 1978.

Tannenbaum, R., & Schmidt, W. H. How to choose a leadership pattern. *Harvard Business Review,* 1958, *3,* 95–101.

Taylor, C. W., & Barron, F. X. *Scientific creativity: Its recognition and development.* New York: Wiley, 1963.

Thompson, J. D., & Tuden, A. Strategies, structures, and processes or organizational decision. In J. D. Thompson & A. Tuden (Eds.), *Comparative studies in administration.* Pittsburgh: University of Pittsburgh Press, 1959.

Tichy, Noel. *Strategic human resource management.* New York: Wiley, 1983.

Torrance, E. P. Scientific views of creativity and factors affecting its growth. *Daedalus,* 1965, *94,* 663–682.

von Oech, Roger. *A whack on the side of the head.* New York: Warner, 1983.

von Oech, Roger. *A kick in the seat of the pants.* New York: Harper & Row, 1986.

Vroom, V. H., & Yetton, P. W. *Leadership and decision making.* Pittsburgh: University of Pittsburgh Press, 1973.

Vygotsky, L. Thought and language. Cambridge, Mass.: MIT Press, 1962.

Watzlawick, P., Weakland, J., & Fisch, R. *Change.* New York: Norton, 1974.

Weick, K. E. *The social psychology of organizing.* Reading, Mass.: Addison-Wesley, 1979.

ACKNOWLEDGMENTS

Solving Problems Creatively

p. 22–24 From *How Creative Are You?* by Eugene Raudsepp. Copyright © 1981 by Eugene Raudsepp. Reprinted by permission.

p. 24–25 Innovative Attitude Scale from "Innovative Attitudes, Values, and Intentions in Organizations" by John E. Ettlie and Robert D. O'Keefe from *Journal of Management Studies,* 1982, *19:*163–182. Reprinted by permission of Basil Blackwell Ltd.

p. 41 "The Shakespeare Riddle," reprinted by permission of the Putnam Publishing Group from *Creative Growth Games* by Eugene Raudsepp and George P. Hough, Jr. Copyright © 1977 by Eugene Raudsepp and George P. Hough, Jr.

p. 42, 45 The Block Problem and Embedded Patterns. From *Experiences in Visual Thinking* by R. H. McKim. Copyright © 1972 by Wadsworth Publishing Company, Inc. Reprinted by permission of Brooks/Cole Publishing Company, Monterey, California.

p. 68–71 Admiral Kimmel's Failure at Pearl Harbor. Reprinted with permission of The Free Press, a division of Macmillan, Inc. From *Decision Making: A Psychological Analysis of Conflict, Choice, and Commitment* by Irving L. Janis and Leon Mann. Copyright © 1977 by The Free Press.

p. 71–73 The Sony Walkman. Reprinted with permission of Rawson Associates, an imprint of Macmillan Publishing Company and W. H. Allen & Co., PLC, from *Breakthroughs!* by John Ketteringham and Ranganath Nayak, p. 130, 134–35. Copyright © 1986 Arthur D. Little, Inc.

p. 75–80 Keith Dunn and McGuffey's Restaurant. From "The Odyssey of an Excellent Man" by Joshua Hyatt. Reprinted with permission, *Inc.* magazine, February 1989. Copyright © 1989 by Goldhirsh Group, Inc., 38 Commercial Wharf, Boston, Mass. 02110.

INDEX